James Mavor, Leo Tolstoy, Vladimir Grigorevich Chertkov

Christian Martyrdom in Russia

James Mavor, Leo Tolstoy, Vladimir Grigorevich Chertkov

Christian Martyrdom in Russia

ISBN/EAN: 9783337715595

Printed in Europe, USA, Canada, Australia, Japan

Cover: Foto ©Andreas Hilbeck / pixelio.de

More available books at **www.hansebooks.com**

CHRISTIAN MARTYRDOM IN RUSSIA

An Account of the MEMBERS of the
UNIVERSAL BROTHERHOOD or

DOUKHOBÓRTSI

now migrating from the
CAUCASUS to CANADA

Edited by
VLADIMIR TCHERTKOFF

Containing a Concluding Chapter and Letter by
LEO TOLSTOY

With an Introduction by
JAMES MAVOR

TORONTO
GEORGE N MORANG
1899

CHRISTIAN MARTYRDOM IN RUSSIA

An Account of the MEMBERS of the UNIVERSAL BROTHERHOOD or

DOUKHOBÒRTSI

now migrating from the
CAUCASUS to CANADA

Edited by
VLADIMIR TCHERTKOFF

Containing a Concluding Chapter and Letter by
LEO TOLSTOY

With an Introduction by
JAMES MAVOR

TORONTO
GEORGE N MORANG
1899

INTRODUCTION

Although this book contains a prefatory note by Mr. Vladimir Tchertkoff for Russian readers, and a preface by Mr. Kenworthy for English readers, I have been asked to write an introduction for readers in Canada and the United States. There is a certain advantage in this because the story may thus be brought down to date. The Doukhobòrtsi (Spirit-Wrestlers)[1] or as they prefer to call themselves, Members of the Universal Brotherhood, seem to have originated as a separate sect in a village on the southern frontier of Russia in the middle of the eighteenth century[2]. Their doctrines infected other peasants in other parts of Russia, and ere long attracted the attention of the Government and of the dignitaries of the Orthodox Greek Church. A number of the sectaries were banished to Siberia, some of them making small settlements on the borders of Manchuria, where, it may be mentioned, their descendants were visited by Prince Kropotkin while he was aide-de-camp to the Governor-General of Eastern Siberia about 1868.

---

[1] Doukhobòrtsi, (Spirit-Wrestlers) is a mere nickname.

[2] An account of their doctrines and their mode of life at the beginning of this century is given in an interesting paper written in 1805. See page 16 *infra*.

INTRODUCTION

In the reign of Alexander I., a tract of land on the northern shore of the Sea of Azov was set apart as a kind of Doukhobor Reserve, and an agricultural commonwealth was established by them under the leadership of an ex-sergeant of the Russian army, called Kapùstin. Kapùstin is described as having "governed them with a practical sense amounting to genius"[1]. Here the Members of the Universal Brotherhood lived for more than fifty years undisturbed. The idea of isolating the Doukhobors was evidently intended to put a stop to their proselitising tendencies, but on these manifesting themselves, notwithstanding their comparative seclusion, their leader Kapùstin was arrested and the community broken up. Since then their doctrines have been held by at most at any one time about 20,000 peasants in various villages in southern Russia. Their religious beliefs have all along been similar to those of the Society of Friends[2]. From time to time the attention of the Government and of the ecclesiastical authorities has been drawn to them. The Government objected to them on

[1] Anatole Leroy-Beaulieu "The Empire of the Czars," New York, 1896, vol. 3, p. 442.

[2] M. Leroy-Beaulieu gives an excellent account of the Doukhobòrtsi especially of their religious beliefs; and a good account is also given by Albert F. Heard "The Russian Church and Russian Dissent," New York, 1887.

A general idea of their present religious views can be obtained from Mr. Tchertkoff's account *infra*. An interesting description of their religious worship is given by T. B. Hussey in "American

account of their refusal to render military service; while the ecclesiastical authorities disapproved of their principles and practices because these are opposed to those of the Orthodox Greek Church.

In consequence of this disapproval the people have been subject to repeated banishments, and their prosperous homes have again and again been broken up. In 1840 and in 1850 they were banished to Trans-Caucasia near the Turkish frontier. For some years they were allowed to live their life there without molestation, and though the inhospitable climate of the Caucasus produced a high rate of mortality, yet some of the villages were exceedingly prosperous, particularly those in the neighbourhood of Kars where they are said to have cultivated their land with such assiduity as greatly to increase the product of the soil.

Up to 1887 the Russian Government administered the conscription laws with comparative laxity, and in consequence non-resisting peasant sects were allowed to remain in comparative immunity, and during this period many of them became the pioneers of Russian colonization[1]. From 1887 onward, however, the military necessities of Russia compelled the authorities to carry out the conscription laws with greater stringency, and then began the series of recent persecutions, especially of the Doukhobòrtsi,

Friend," Philadelphia, copied in "Friends' Intelligencer," Philadelphia, 12th mo. 3, 1898, p. 884.

[1] Leroy-Beaulieu, "The Empire of the Czars," vol. 3, p. 443.

which have led to the present situation as described in this book. The attitude of the sect towards the demands of the Government was for the most part a steadfast one, but there were some backsliders. In 1895 the "Great Party" or those who adhered rigidly to the traditional tenets of the sect made up its mind to destroy its offensive weapons, and these were formally burned on the night of the 28th of June, in Tiflis, Elisavetpol, and in Kars. This was taken as a sign of rebellion and the persecutions became more vigorous. In 1897, Mr. Tchertkoff, the author of this book, who was formerly an officer in the Russian army, visited St. Petersburg, and had an interview with Mr. Pobiédonòstseff, the High Procurator of the Holy Synod, the result of which was an intimation to himself that it would be convenient for him if he withdrew from Russia. The visit of the Empress Maria, the mother of the present Czar, to the Caucasus was, however, taken advantage of by the Doukhobors and their sympathizers and their case was put before her. It is understood that the Dowager Empress enlisted the sympathies of the Czar and secured for the Doukhobors permission to leave the country. This permission was given in February, 1898[1], and then the Doukhobors immediately began to make assiduous enquiries

---

[1] The following is a copy of the official notification:—

"The Fasting-Doukhobòrtsi, who were expelled in 1895 from the district of Akhalkalak, and transported into other districts of the Government of Tiflis, having submitted a petition to her

INTRODUCTION

about suitable places to which they might emigrate. They had been accustomed to agriculture, principally corn growing, and to a dry climate with cold winters. At first they thought of Cyprus, which is now being colonized under the care of an English Cyprus Colonization Committee. Proposals were also made about other places.

On the 28th of March, that is a month after formal permission had been given to emigrate, the Doukhobors telegraphed to Mr. Tchertkoff at Purleigh in Essex, England, for help and advice. The

> Imperial Majesty, the Empress Maria Feodorovna, asking either to be grouped and settled into one place, and to be exempt from the duties of military service, or to be allowed to emigrate, the following instructions have been received:—
>
> "1. The request for exemption from military service is refused.
>
> "2. The Fasting-Doukhobòrtsi—with the exception, of course, of those who have reached the age at which they can be summoned to the duties of military service, and of those who have failed to fulfil those duties—may emigrate under these conditions:—(a) That they provide themselves with a foreign passport, in accordance with the established order; (b) that they leave the frontiers of Russia at their own expense; and (c) that before leaving they sign an agreement never to return within the borders of the empire, understanding that in the case of non-compliance with this last point the offender will be condemned to exile to remote places.
>
> " As to their request to be settled in one village, it is refused.
>
> "This notification is issued by order of the Governor of Tiflis to one of the petitioning Fasting-Doukhobòrtsi, Vassili Potapoff, in answer to his personal application.
>
> "Tiflis, Feb. 21, 1898."

Society of Friends in England had liberally aided the Doukhobors during the three preceding years, and it was only natural that they should be again approached on the subject. The matter was brought before the Meeting for Sufferings, a committee was formed, and later an appeal was issued. Simultaneously the small community at Purleigh, consisting of sympathizers with the teachings of Count Tolstoy, formed a committee consisting of V. Tchertkoff, P. Biriukoff, A. Gilvart (Professor of Royal College of Science, London), H. P. Archer (late Secretary of the Brotherhood Church, Croydon), and two or three others. In order to make inquiry Mr. Tchertkoff had sent to the Caucasus an ex-Captain of the British army, Mr. St. John, who had been expelled from Russia on account of these inquiries. It was, therefore, thought to be expedient for a deputation from the Doukhobors to come to England for the purpose of supplying the information necessary for the best kind of action under the circumstances. Ivan Ivin and P. Makhartoff therefore came with their families to England, and the committees were then made aware of the state of the case. It appeared that about 3,500 of the people were comparatively well off and that they had a considerable common fund besides the emigration fund, which they had succeeded in raising specially. In addition to these about 3,000 were, though not possessed of very ample resources, still not destitute. They also had a common fund and a

INTRODUCTION

fund for purposes of emigration. There were, however, about 2,000 who were much worse off than the previous sections, 1,000 of them being in very urgent need of assistance.

In view of these circumstances an arrangement was made with the Cyprus Colonization Committee to receive 1,100 of those in most urgent need. Cyprus was chosen, not because it was the most suitable place for colonization, but because it was the nearest. The British Government demanded, however, a guarantee of £15 ($75) each before permission would be granted to land. Within a few days the Society of Friends, with the greatest magnanimity, provided the whole of this amount, about $75,000. The 1,100 were then landed in Cyprus. From reports since received they have done fairly well there this summer, although it would appear that the rent charged to them by the Cyprus Colonization Committee was rather higher than perhaps the circumstances warranted. There thus remained to be dealt with 3,500 persons whose case was not very specially urgent, and between 2,000 and 3,000 whose case, as regards some of them at any rate, was very urgent indeed. Various places had been suggested, and offers had been received from the Argentine and from Brazil, as well as from Texas and California; but the state of chronic disturbance in which the South American Republics were known to be involved, and the prevalence of a war feeling in the United States were discouraging elements to people, one of whose leading principles was objection to military service. While the committee at Purleigh, who had received full authority from the Doukhobòrtsi to act for them, were puzzling themselves to know what to do, one of their number happened to read in the *Nineteenth Century* an article by Prince Kropotkin upon the resources of Canada and particularly upon the Mennonite settlement in Manitoba, which he visited in the autumn of 1897 when in Canada as a member of the British Association. In July they wrote to Prince Kropotkin asking him for further information. He at once paid a visit to Purleigh and put them into communication with persons in Canada. The matter was placed before the Government, and the present immigration is the result.

In order that the Doukhobors might be fully aware of the conditions in Canada, the two families who had come to England to give and to get information, arrived in Montreal in September, 1898. They were accompanied by Prince Hilkoff, the nephew of the Russian Minister of Railways, who found himself much in sympathy with their religious views, particularly with their attitude towards militarism, and by Mr. Aylmer Maude, who had been a merchant in Moscow, and who had met the Doukhobors at Purleigh. This deputation went to Edmonton, and to other districts in the North-West, for the purpose of inspecting the country.

There were three special reasons why the emi-

INTRODUCTION 11

gration should be conducted as speedily as possible. One was that the resources which the people had were being dissipated by fines and removals in consequence of the action of the authorities. Secondly, the people were anxious to take advantage of the permission to emigrate so long as the government adhered to the permission. How long this would last no one could tell. Thirdly, the annual conscription takes place on the 1st of January, and those young men who have reached the statutory age are then drawn into the army. These considerations rendered it advisable that those of the Doukhobors to whom they applied should be aided in leaving the country without delay. The number thus to be dealt with turned out to be about 2,000. Steps were taken to provide the necessary supplement to their own funds. Count Leo Tolstoy sold three short stories to a Russian publisher, and the proceeds, about $5,000, were remitted to the Purleigh Committee. The Society of Friends in England, the individual members of the committee at Purleigh, and the Society of Friends at Philadelphia, have altogether supplied the means for the emigration of this contingent, which comprises the poorest of the Doukhobor groups. After delays, in consequence of the difficulty of obtaining a steamer direct from Batoum to Canada, about 1,822 have now at latest advices embarked at Batoum on December 22nd on board the Beaver Line steamer *Lake Huron* direct for St John N.B. They will probably reach this country in the second or third week in January. A further contingent is expected to sail by the *Lake Superior* of the same line about the beginning of the year; while the remainder will probably sail in February or March, 1899. The first party is being accompanied by Count Serge Tolstoy, son of Count Leo Tolstoy.

The land which has been granted to them by the Government is situated north-east and south-west of Fort Pelly, and occupies an angle at the extreme north-west corner of the Province of Manitoba, where it adjoins the North-West Territories. The district is known as the Swan River District, and is believed to be suitable for settlement of this character. Since it would be impracticable for the emigrants to take up their permanent habitation in the depth of winter, it has been arranged by the Government that those who come out in January shall be temporarily housed at various points where the Government have suitable buildings or buildings which could be made suitable[1].

[1] Mr. W. F. McCreary, Commissioner of Immigration at Winnipeg, gives the following particulars of the methods which will be adopted in effecting the settlement of the people upon the land : " Sixty picked Doukhobors will be sent from Yorkton, and a like number from Dauphin, with a full equipment of tools, horses, oxen, sleighs and provisions, who will at once proceed to the respective reserves, and at once commence cutting timber for the erection of storehouses, for supplies and houses for families.... I expect the Doukhobors to plant about forty acres of potatoes in each colony [there are two], besides large quantities of other

INTRODUCTION

A Committee has been formed at Winnipeg for the purpose of making arrangements for their comfort during the winter and subsequent settlement in the spring. The members of this Committee are Mr. Thomas McCaffrey, Manager of the Union Bank of Canada; Mr. D. W. Bole, wholesale merchant and President of the Board of Trade of Winnipeg, and Prince Hilkoff, and one other yet to be named. Mr. Alexander Moffatt, accountant, Winnipeg, will act as secretary of the committee. Those of the emigrants who arrive in January will be maintained during the winter by means of funds at the disposal of the Committee, and in the spring the remainder of the people, including probably those who had gone to Cyprus, will be settled upon the Reserves. The total number will probably be about 8,500. In addition to the English and Winnipeg committees, there has been formed in Philadelphia a committee of the Society of Friends there; and in New York an influential committee of friends and sympathizers of Count Leo Tolstoy are also collecting subscriptions with a view to the comfortable establishment of the Doukhobors upon their Reserves. The members of the New York Com-

---

vegetables; also rye, barley, flax and some wheat. Next summer land will be prepared for a large wheat crop the ensuing summer, also for oats, and sufficient hay will be made for their stock of all kinds. Arrangements have been made whereby any of the men not required for work in the colony will get abundant employment on railway construction."—W. F. McCreary in "Friends' Intelligencer," Philadelphia, 12th mo. 24, 1898, p. 942.

mittee are : Messrs. Wm. Dean Howells, New York ; Miss Jane Addams, Chicago ; Wm. Lloyd Garrison, Boston ; Geo. Dana Boardman, D.D., Philadelphia ; N. O. Nelson, St. Louis ; Bolton Hall, New York ; Ernest H. Crosby, New York ; and Isaac N. Seligman, Treasurer, New York. About $5,000 have already been subscribed in America.

Since a guarantee of immunity from military service was an indispensable condition of settlement, the Government has agreed to place by Order-in-Council the Doukhobors on the same footing as the Mennonites, members of the Society of Friends, and Tunkers who already possess statutory exemption from being called upon to render military service.

It remains to notice that the members of the Universal Brotherhood practise practical communism within the group[1]. This communism arose from

---

[1] Prince Hilkoff informs me that this system of community of goods dates only from 1893.

Mr. Tchertkoff gives in a private letter the following interesting account of their communal life :—

"In their normal condition the Doukhobòrtsi have in each village a common workshop fitted up with tools mostly of their own making, where carpenters, blacksmiths, etc., labour at what is necessary for the community. If anything is wanted, therefore, notice is given at the workshop. When asked whether this work was paid for they seemed astonished at the idea. If the supply exceeds the demand, sometimes the goods are sold to outsiders, but not much of this is done. They sell corn and produce sufficient to enable them to pay taxes and procure articles they are not able to make for themselves. Before this last pressure of persecution they were all comfortably off, and had a large common the necessity of self-protection. They felt that they could secure this, most effectually, by means of a unity of economic interest. Each group consists of about 140 or 150 families, and each group holds its property in common. There is no trading within the group; but they sell their surplus products for the common benefit of the members of it. Although each group has thus its independent property, and the

fund, which latter, however, was stolen from them through the intrigues of false brethren, assisted by the authorities. The women weave their own cloth and are fond of embroidering their garments. They have a costume of their own, differing slightly from the ordinary Russian peasant. The children are very quick and intelligent, and those now in England are learning very rapidly. These people are very cleanly in their habits, and most courteous and dignified in their behaviour, grateful for every kindness, tender and sympathetic. In their own villages they are always ready to welcome strangers, and ask no payment. Their honesty in the markets is unquestioned by all who know them, and the government even bears witness to their good character."

They are vegetarians (having become so in 1893), total abstainers, and non-smokers; although every individual is at liberty to do as he pleases, so far as the doctrines of the sect are concerned. These inculcate only frugality.

In reply to inquiries regarding the character of the Doukhobors, Count Leo Tolstoy writes as follows:—

"1. The Doukhobórtsi are the best farmers of Russia.

"2. They would use land and seeds given to them in the best way.

"3. They live the most chaste family life.

"4. They would adapt themselves to any climate.

"5. They would send their children to the common school if the children would not be obliged to receive religious teaching."

groups are not equally well off, it is the habit for the groups to help each other in case of need. The most interesting points connected with this emigration are: first, that the people are not leaving their own country because they have been failures in an economic sense there, but because of their opposition to the autocratic militarism of Russia; second, that their industry and frugality have always, wherever they have been settled, resulted in prosperity.

The need for assistance which has already so largely and so generously been granted to them, has arisen from the suddenness and the magnitude of the movement, and also from the circumstance that in leaving their villages they have been obliged to abandon a considerable part of the results of their industry.

The similarity of the climate and the soil of the North-West of Canada to those of South Russia suggests that the emigrants will be able, without undue hardship to themselves, to bring into cultivation a region of this country, which, while possessed of great natural fertility, yet offers small attraction for any but those who have a special attitude for the function of pioneering.

JAMES MAVOR

University of Toronto
December 20th 1898

CHRISTIAN MARTYRDOM
IN RUSSIA

CHRISTIAN MARTYRDOM
IN RUSSIA

*PERSECUTION OF THE SPIRIT-WRESTLERS
(OR DOUKHOBORTSI) IN THE CAUCASUS*

EDITED BY

VLADIMIR TCHERTKOFF

CONTAINING A CONCLUDING CHAPTER AND LETTER

BY

LEO TOLSTOY

Fifth Thousand

LONDON:
THE BROTHERHOOD PUBLISHING CO.
26 PATERNOSTER SQUARE, E.C.
1897

THE readers of this book will see that the suffering Spirit-Wrestlers have at the present moment been brought to the last extremity of need, their own means being by this time entirely exhausted. Every donation, therefore, on their behalf, would now be specially acceptable, and may be sent to

VLADIMIR TCHERTKOFF,

BROOMFIELD, DUPPAS HILL,

CROYDON.

The profits from this edition will be added to the general fund for the help of the Spirit-Wrestlers.

TABLE OF CONTENTS

	PAGE
PREFACE. By J. C. KENWORTHY.	vii
PREFATORY NOTE FOR RUSSIAN READERS. By VLADIMIR TCHERTKOFF	ix

CHAPTER I
THE SPIRIT-WRESTLERS 1

CHAPTER II
THE SPIRIT-WRESTLERS ONE HUNDRED YEARS AGO . 16

CHAPTER III
THE CHARACTER AND PRINCIPLES OF THE SPIRIT-WRESTLERS TO-DAY 36

CHAPTER IV
MILITARY PRISONERS LEBEDEFF AND COMPANIONS . 50

CHAPTER V
THE BURNING OF ARMS JUNE 1895, AND "THE EXECUTION" 57

CHAPTER VI
CONSCRIPTION, ARRESTS, IMPRISONMENTS, EXILE . . 65

CHAPTER VII
PRESENT CONDITION OF THOSE WHO WERE BANISHED, ETC. 79

CHAPTER VIII
CONCLUSION BY LEO TOLSTOY 92

APPENDIX I
LETTER FROM PETER VERIGIN TO THE EMPRESS ALEXANDRA FEODOROVNA 101

APPENDIX II
LETTER FROM LEO TOLSTOY TO THE COMMANDER OF THE EKATERINOGRAD PENAL BATTALION . . . 104

APPENDIX III
EXTRACT FROM LETTER FROM VLADIMIR TCHERTKOFF TO THE SAME 107

PREFACE

I AM asked to write some words to English readers, by way of preface to this book.

What feeling would I most wish to awaken in the mind of an English reader, before he reads? Certainly, the feeling that these Russian Doukhobortsi (Spirit-Wrestlers), persecuted and martyred simply because they are too good to be understood by the mass of their fellowmen—are of the reader's own flesh and blood. Their sufferings and their needs ought to call upon each of us, as would the sufferings and the needs of our own brothers and sisters.

It is true the Doukhobortsi are, or until recently have been, quite obscure, an unknown peasant sect of the Caucasus. But why have they been obscure? For the same reason that the present life and past history of all such people is made obscure; because they are men of sincere religion, who esteem it their duty to live by those Christian principles which the most of us profess with our lips, and entirely violate in our lives. They are a light shining in darkness—in darkness which moves actively to hide and smother the light.

It will seem incredible to many of us that the things here recorded can by any possibility be true, in this the nineteenth Christian century. Men, women and children have been beaten, imprisoned, abused, robbed, exiled, starved to death, by scores and thousands. The perpetrators of these—shall we say "crimes" or "excesses"?—are men who help to form the government of an empire which calls itself "holy"—Holy Russia,—in the Christian sense. The victims are people whose sole fault is the practice of the Christian virtues of a pure worship of God, communism of goods, and peace—"non-resistance to evil." All these circumstances are attested in this book, by the direct and indirect evidence of men, whose honesty of purpose and scrupulous exactitude are shown by the very manner of their speaking.

Surely the modern State condemns itself immediately and completely, when it thus brings itself into direct and destructive enmity with people whose beliefs and lives are precisely calculated to promote the ends which the State so hypocritically assumes to serve—the ends of social justice and well-being. This book should be received by us as a record of the deeds and sufferings of people, who, in another country, are casting their lives against that common enemy, the rule of brute force in society. Those who sincerely and intelligently desire the passing away of "the kingdom of this world," and the coming of "the kingdom of heaven," will acknowledge the Doukhobortsi as their brethren, martyrs in the cause.

And such people will not be slow to help. Food, clothing and shelter are needed for the remnant of the sufferers; those who have it in their hearts to give will give.

But let it be remembered that no appeal for help has been, or is, made by the Doukhobortsi themselves. They say that God, Who is their life, will send what they need, and they are content to suffer, if it be His will, in the persuasion that all the persecution in the world cannot take from them the eternal life, which is theirs through obedience to the truth. They say that the best thing a man can do is to give his life to the service of the spirit shown forth by Jesus, who said, "Love one another. Love your enemies."

All those who are concerned in the production of this book, from Leo Tolstoy to the last of the peasants whose letters are quoted, would join in so saying; feeling that the first mission of the book is, to let the world know how the life of truth is growing by suffering in its midst.

JOHN C. KENWORTHY.

LONDON, *August* 1897.

PREFATORY NOTE FOR RUSSIAN READERS

As this book will probably be read, not only by Englishmen, but also by Russians, I should like, in a few introductory remarks, to remove a misunderstanding which is likely to arise in the minds of some Russian readers concerning the motives which have prompted its publication.

The contents of this book may produce upon a certain class of my countrymen the unpleasant impression that, by publishing it abroad and in a foreign language, I am seeking, as it were, to discredit the Russian Government in the eyes of foreigners,—a thing which, in the opinion of these readers, a man who was really attached to his country would never do.

In answer to this, I can only say that I have been exiled from my country for being a friend and co-worker of Leo Tolstoy, and for attempting to disclose the truth concerning certain abuses by the Russian Government, as well to help its innocently-persecuted victims, as for the sake of those representatives of the Government itself, who know not what they do. Since then, living here in exile, I am experiencing the pain inevitably caused by compulsory separation from those of my countrymen who are nearest to my heart, and from the people to whose interests the last fifteen years of my life have been devoted. Finding myself in this position, I am naturally not able—notwithstanding all my desire to admit my mistakes and failures—in sincerity to convict myself of indifference to my country.

But neither can I identify with my country that governmental system which is causing it to suffer so severely.

And, indeed, why should I conceal from myself and others the fact, acknowledged by all except the deluded or prejudiced upholders of the State organisation of Russia, that it is difficult to imagine a system more soulless, senseless and savage, more cowardly, deceitful and cruel, than the present Russian Government, together with the mercenary Church which supports it?[1]

Wishing my country true welfare, I cannot but hope and look for the coming of that day when the representatives of the Government, on the one hand, will awaken to the consciousness of the moral unlawfulness of that arbitrary system of uncontrolled brute force in which they now participate; and, on the other hand, the Russian people and society will realise the truth, that the first and most sacred duty of every man, before God and before his fellow-creatures, is to cease to fulfil those demands of Church and State which are contrary to his conscience.

My native country I love, because I cannot help loving it. But I love it not with that blind prejudice which seeks to justify all its dark and humiliating iniquities; I love it without shutting my eyes to all the atrocities perpetrated in it and to all the sufferings of its oppressed masses. Such prejudice would not be love, but patriotic vanity,—a sentiment which always does immeasurable harm to the nation towards which it is directed. Loving my country, I try to love and appreciate in it that which is highest and best.

And this highest manifestation of truth and righteousness in my country, I cannot fail to see in that revival of pure Christianity which is now taking place in various corners of the land, and which is undergoing the most cruel persecution

---

[1] I feel it necessary to remark that, in thus alluding to the Russian Government, I in no wise have in view its nominal directors, the Emperors,—men often remarkably conscientious and well-intentioned, but who in reality belong to the category of victims of the Government being, in consequence of their peculiar position, deprived of the possibility of free and independent action. Of all the unfortunate dupes of the Government, they are the most deluded, and therefore, in a certain sense, of all its representatives the least influential and the most helpless. And indeed it cannot be otherwise as long as the so-called autocratic form of government is maintained in Russia, with its necessary absence of publicity and of freedom of speech.

at the hands of a Government, desirous of systematically wiping off the face of the earth thousands of human beings, whose only crime is that they acknowledge all men to be their brothers, regard no one as their enemy, and therefore refuse to kill anyone.

At the same time, I am firmly convinced that for the welfare of humanity it is important that all should know of these bright examples of true Christianity, however remote and inaccessible may be the locality in which they are manifested. It is such examples alone that will effectively promote international peace and universal disarmament, which are, in words at least, so generally desired, and the possibility of which is doubted by those only whose lives are founded upon that same general armament and violence, which render the perfect development of love and goodwill among men impossible.

Firmly believing that the conduct of the Spirit-Wrestlers is furthering the coming of the Kingdom of God upon earth, and at the same time knowing that the more widely the truth is spread concerning the condition of these brothers of mine, who are being martyred for conscience' sake, so much the more difficult will it become for the local authorities to continue their atrocities and murders,—could I refrain from sharing with as many people as possible the information I have succeeded in collecting concerning this matter?

And is it surprising that, having been forced to leave my country precisely for having attempted to express aloud the truth in Russia, and in Russian, I, who believe in the mutual brotherhood of all nations, have, for the attainment of my aim, profited by the liberty of conscience and of speech enjoyed by the country which at present affords me hospitality?

VLADIMIR TCHERTKOFF.

CROYDON, *August 9th*, 1897.

CHRISTIAN MARTYRDOM IN RUSSIA

I

THE SPIRIT-WRESTLERS

A TERRIBLE cruelty is now being perpetrated in the Caucasus. More than four thousand people are suffering and dying from hunger, disease, exhaustion, blows, tortures, and other persecutions at the hands of the Russian authorities.

These suffering people are the Doukhobortsi (or "Spirit-Wrestlers") of the Caucasus. They are enduring persecution, because their religious convictions do not allow them to fulfil those demands of the State which are connected, directly or indirectly, with the killing of, or violence to, their fellow-men.

[Thus ran the introduction to an Appeal signed by Paul Birukoff, John Tregouboff, and Vladimir Tchertkoff, and issued in Russia 12th December 1896. The Appeal continues:—]

Brief and fragmentary notices of these remarkable people have not unfrequently appeared of late in the Russian and foreign press. But all that has been published in the Russian newspapers has been either too short, or in a mutilated form,—whether intentionally, unintentionally, or as a concession to the requirements of the Russian censor,—while what has been printed abroad is, unfortunately, little accessible to the Russian public. Hence it is that we consider it our duty in this Appeal to give a general view of the events that are now taking place, and a brief sketch of the circumstances which preceded them.

[The same also is the object of this book, therefore we cannot do better than give the Appeal in full.]

The Spirit-Wrestlers first appeared in the middle of last century. By the end of the last century or the beginning of the present, their doctrine had become so clearly defined, and the number of their followers had so greatly increased, that the Government and the Church, considering this sect to be peculiarly obnoxious, started a cruel persecution.

The foundation of the Spirit-Wrestlers' teaching

consists in the belief that the Spirit of God is present in the soul of man, and directs him by its word within him.

They understand the coming of Christ in the flesh, His works, teaching, and sufferings, in a spiritual sense. The object of the sufferings of Christ, in their view, was to give us an example of suffering for truth. Christ continues to suffer in us even now, when we do not live in accordance with the behests and spirit of His teaching. The whole teaching of the Spirit-Wrestlers is penetrated with the gospel spirit of love.

Worshipping God in the spirit, the Spirit-Wrestlers affirm that the outward Church and all that is performed in it and concerns it has no importance for them. The Church is where two or three are gathered together, *i.e.* united, in the name of Christ.

They pray inwardly at all times; while, on fixed days (corresponding for convenience to the orthodox holy-days), they assemble for prayer-meetings, at which they read prayers and sing hymns, or psalms as they call them, and greet each other fraternally with low bows, thereby acknowledging every man as a bearer of the Divine Spirit.

The teaching of the Spirit-Wrestlers is founded on tradition. This tradition is called among them the "Book of Life," because it lives in their memory and hearts. It consists of psalms, partly formed out of the contents of the Old and New Testaments, partly composed independently.

The Spirit-Wrestlers found alike their mutual relations and their relations to other people—and not only to people, but to all living creatures—exclusively on love; and, therefore, they hold all people equal, brethren. They extend this idea of equality also to the Government authorities; obedience to whom they do not consider binding upon them in those cases when the demands of these authorities are in conflict with their conscience; while, in all that does not infringe what they regard as the will of God, they willingly fulfil the desire of the authorities.

They consider murder, violence, and in general all relations to living beings not based on love, as opposed to their conscience, and to the will of God.

The Spirit-Wrestlers are industrious and abstemious in their lives, and always truthful in their speech, accounting all lying a great sin.

Such, in their most general character, are the beliefs for which the Spirit-Wrestlers have long endured cruel persecution.

The Emperor Alexander I., in one of his rescripts concerning the Spirit-Wrestlers, dated the

THE SPIRIT-WRESTLERS

9th December 1816, expressed himself as follows:—
"All the measures of severity exhausted upon the Spirit-Wrestlers during the thirty years up to 1801, not only did not destroy this sect, but more and more multiplied the number of its adherents." And therefore he proposed more humane treatment of them. But, notwithstanding this desire of the Emperor, the persecutions did not cease. Under Nicholas I. they were particularly enforced, and by his command, in the years '40 and '50 the Spirit-Wrestlers were all banished from the government of Tauris, where they were formerly settled, to Transcaucasia, near the Turkish frontier. "The utility of this measure is evident," says a previous resolution of the Committee of Ministers of the 6th February 1826, "they [the Spirit-Wrestlers] being transported to the extreme borders of the Caucasus, and being always confronted by the hillsmen, must of necessity protect their property and families by force of arms," *i.e.* they would have to renounce their convictions. Moreover the place appointed for their settlement, the so-called Wet Hills, was one (situated in what is now the Ahalkalaky district of the Tiflis government) having a severe climate, standing 5000 feet above the sea-level, in which barley grows with difficulty, and where the crops are often destroyed by frost. Others of the Spirit-Wrestlers

were planted in the present government of Elisavetpol.

But neither the severe climate nor the neighbourhood of wild and warlike hillsmen shook the faith of the Spirit-Wrestlers, who, in the course of the half-century they passed in the Wet Hills, transformed this wilderness into flourishing colonies, and continued to live the same Christian and laborious life they had lived before. But, as nearly always happens with people, the temptation of the wealth which they attained to in the Caucasus weakened their moral force, and little by little they began to depart somewhat from the requirements of their belief.

But, while temporarily departing, in the external relations of life, from the claims of their conscience, they did not, in their inner consciousness, renounce the basis of their beliefs; and, therefore, as soon as events happened among them which disturbed their outward tranquillity, the religious spirit which had guided their fathers immediately revived within them.

In 1887, universal military service was introduced in the Caucasus; and even those for whom it was formerly (in consideration of their religious convictions) replaced by other service or by banishment, were called upon to serve. This measure took the Spirit-Wrestlers unawares, and at first they outwardly submitted to it; but they never in their consciences renounced the belief that war is a great sin, and they exhorted their sons taken as recruits, though they submitted to the various regulations of the service, never to make actual use of their arms. Nevertheless, the introduction of the conscription among people who considered every murder and act of violence against their fellow-men to be a sin, greatly alarmed them, and caused them to think over the degree to which they had departed from their belief.

At the same time, in consequence of an illegal decision of the Government departments and officials, the right to the possession of the public property of the Spirit-Wrestlers (valued at half a million roubles) passed from the community to one of their members, who, for his own personal advantage, had betrayed the public interest. This called forth the protest of the majority of the Spirit-Wrestlers against this individual and his party, who had thus become possessed of the public property, and against the corrupt local administration, which had been bribed to give an unjust decision in the case.

When, besides this, several representatives of the majority, and among them the manager elected to administer the communal property, were banished to the government of Archangel, this awakening assumed a very definite character.

The majority of the Spirit-Wrestlers (about twelve thousand in number) resolved to hold fast to the traditions left them by their fathers. They renounced tobacco, wine, meat, and every kind of excess, divided up all their property (thus supplying the needs of those who were then in want), and they collected a new public fund.

In connection with this return to a strictly Christian life, they also renounced all participation in acts of violence, and therefore refused military service.

In confirmation of the sincerity of their decision not to use violence even for their own defence, in the summer of 1895 the Spirit-Wrestlers of the "Great Party," as they were called, burnt all their arms which they, like all the inhabitants of the Caucasus, kept for their protection, and those who were in the army refused to continue service. By general resolution they fixed on the night of 28th June for the purpose of burning their arms, which were their own property and therefore at their absolute disposal. This holocaust was accompanied by the singing of psalms, and was carried out simultaneously in three places, namely:—in the governments of Tiflis and Elisavetpol and in the territory of Kars. In the latter district it passed off without interference; in the government of Elisavetpol it resulted in the imprisonment of forty Spirit-Wrestlers, who are still in confinement; while in the government of Tiflis the action taken by the local administration resulted in the perpetration by the troops of a senseless, unprovoked, and incredibly savage attack on these defenceless people, and in their cruel ill-treatment.

The burning of arms in the Tiflis government was appointed to take place near the village of Goreloe, inhabited by Spirit-Wrestlers belonging to the " Small Party," in whose hands was the public property they had appropriated. This party having learnt the intention of the " Great Party " to burn their weapons, were either afraid of such an assembly, or wished to slander them, and informed the authorities that the Spirit-Wrestlers of the " Great Party " were devising a rising and preparing to make an armed attack upon the village of Goreloe. The local authorities, then, without verifying the truth of this information, ordered out the Cossacks and infantry to the place of the imaginary riot. The Cossacks arrived at the place of assembly of the Spirit-Wrestlers in the morning, when the bonfire, which had destroyed their arms, was already burning out, and they made two cavalry attacks upon these men and women, who had voluntarily disarmed themselves and were singing hymns, and the troops beat them with their whips in the most inhuman manner.

After this, a whole series of persecutions was commenced against all the Spirit-Wrestlers belonging to the "Great Party." First of all, the troops called out were quartered "in execution" on the Spirit-Wrestlers' settlements, *i.e.* the property and the inhabitants themselves of these settlements were placed at the disposal of the officers, soldiers, and Cossacks quartered in these villages. Their property was plundered, and the inhabitants themselves were insulted and maltreated in every way, while the women were flogged with whips and some of them violated. The men, numbering about three hundred, who had refused to continue in the army service, and about thirty who had refused active service, were thrown into prison or sent to a penal battalion.

Afterwards more than four hundred families of Spirit-Wrestlers in Ahalkalaky were torn from their prosperous holdings and splendidly cultivated land, and after the forced sale, for a mere trifle, of their property, they were banished from the Ahalkalaky district to four other districts of the Tiflis government, and scattered among the Georgian villages, from one to five families to each village, and there abandoned to their fate.

As early as last autumn, epidemics, such as fevers, typhus, diphtheria and dysentery, appeared among the Spirit-Wrestlers (scattered as above stated), with the result that the mortality increased largely, especially among the children.

THE SPIRIT-WRESTLERS

The Spirit-Wrestlers had been exiled from a cold mountain climate and settled in the hot Caucasian valleys, where even the natives suffer from fevers; and consequently nearly all the Spirit-Wrestlers are sick, partly because (not having dwellings of their own) they are huddled together in hired quarters; but chiefly because they lack means of subsistence.

Their only earnings are from daily labour among the population amidst whom they have been thrown, and beyond the bounds of whose villages they are not allowed to go. But these earnings are very small, the more so that the native population suffered this year both from a bad harvest and from inundations. Those who are settled near the railway pick up something by working there, and share the wages they get with the rest. But this is only a drop in the ocean of their common want.

The material position of the Spirit-Wrestlers is getting worse and worse every day. The exiles have no other food than bread, and sometimes there is a lack of even this. Already among the majority of them certain eye diseases, which are the sure harbingers of scurvy, have appeared.

In one place of exile situated in the Signak district, 106 deaths occurred among 100 families (about 1000 people) settled there. In the Gory district, 147 deaths occurred among 190 families.

In the Tionet district, 83 deaths occurred among 100 families. In the Dushet district, 20 deaths occurred among 72 families. Almost all are suffering from diseases, and disease and mortality are constantly increasing.

Besides these deaths there have been others (due to actual violence) among the Spirit-Wrestlers in prison and in the penal battalion.

The first to die in this way, in July 1895, was Kirill Konkin, the cause of death being blows received as corporal punishment. He died on the road, before reaching the place of his exile, in a state of hallucination, which commenced while he was being flogged. Next, in August 1896, died Michael Scherbinin in the Ekaterinograd penal battalion, tortured to death by flogging, and by being thrown with violence over the wooden horse in the gymnasium. Among those confined in the prisons, many have already died. Some of them, while dying, were locked up in separate rooms, and neither their fellow-prisoners, nor parents, wives and children who had come to bid them farewell, were allowed even to enter the room where the dying lay, alone and helpless. More deaths are to be expected both among the population suffering from want in exile and in the prisons.[1]

---

[1] The information here briefly summarised upon this subject can, in case of need, be supplied in detail, and confirmed

THE SPIRIT-WRESTLERS

The Spirit-Wrestlers themselves do not ask for help—neither those who are in exile with their families, famished, and with starving and sick children, nor those who are being slowly but surely tortured to death in the prisons. They die without uttering a single cry for help, knowing why and for what they suffer. But we, who see these sufferings, and know about them, cannot remain unmoved.

But how to help them?

There are only two means to help people persecuted for faith's sake. One consists in the fulfilment of the Christian commandment, to welcome the stranger, clothe the naked, visit the sick and imprisoned, and feed the hungry, which is prescribed to us both by our own hearts and by the Gospel; the other consists in appealing to the persecutors, both to those who prescribe the persecutions and to those who allow them to take place when they might stop them; and also to those who, without sympathising with the persecutions, participate in them and become their means,—appealing by laying

by the most irrefragable proofs, destroying the whole of the monstrous libels against the Spirit-Wrestlers contained in such statements as the "Confidential Report of Prince Shervashidze, Governor of Tiflis, to General Sheremetieff, the Viceroy of the Caucasus," extracts from which have appeared also in the papers. We keep the whole of the material carefully collected by us, from which the absolute accuracy of our statements may be verified. (Note in the original Appeal.)

bare before these persecutors the sin, the cruelty, and the folly of their acts.

Having been in a position sooner than others to know what has here been set forth, we appeal alike to Russians and to non-Russians to help our brethren in their present sore distress, both with money offerings to relieve the sufferings of the aged, sick, and children, and by raising their voices on behalf of the persecuted.

The most important and grateful means of expressing sympathy with the persecuted, and of softening the hearts of the persecutors, would be personally to visit the victims, in order to see with one's own eyes what is being done with them now, and to make the truth about them generally known.

The expression of sympathy is dear to the Spirit-Wrestlers, because, although they do not ask for help, they yet have no greater joy than to see the manifestation of love and pity to them on the part of others—of that same love for the sake of which these martyrs are sacrificing their lives.

The making publicly known of the truth about the Spirit-Wrestlers is important, because it cannot be that the Russian State authorities really desire to exterminate these people by the inexorable demand from them of that which their conscience does not allow them to do, and the ceaseless persecution and torture of them on this account. There is probably here some misunderstanding, and therefore it is that the promulgation of the truth which may remove this is specially important.

Help!

[This Appeal attained its purpose by drawing the attention both of the public and of the higher authorities to what was being done to the Spirit-Wrestlers by the local authorities of the Caucasus. But for the three friends who signed it, the result was their banishment—two of them, P. Birukoff and J. Tregouboff—to small towns in the Baltic provinces; while V. Tchertkoff was given the choice between the same sentence and being altogether exiled from Russia. He chose the latter as affording him the possibility of helping, from abroad, his persecuted friends, which would have been impossible under the conditions of strict police supervision under which those banished to Russian towns have to live.]

II

THE SPIRIT-WRESTLERS ONE HUNDRED YEARS AGO

A PAPER WRITTEN IN 1805 [1]

IN the second half of the last century there arose in Russia a Society the existence of which would have seemed impossible in our country. Suddenly there appeared people who not only repudiated all the religious ceremonies and outward ritual of the Greek-Russian Church, but even did not accept the outward baptism by water, and the communion of the body and blood of Christ in the bread and wine.

[1] The text is translated from the Russian of an old MS. lately republished in a monthly periodical called *Russian Antiquity*. We have translated it almost in full, as being evidently written by an individual well acquainted, and himself in perfect sympathy, with the religious movement in question. It gives a very fair idea of the life and teaching of the Spirit-Wrestlers at the time indicated, and indeed at the present time. The remarkable events which have happened among this people during the last few years are, in reality, but the result of a revival of their ancient spiritual tendencies, for which they have suffered persecution at the hands of the Church and the Government from the very first.—(Ed.)

It was natural that such men could not have been left in peace, either by their neighbours or by the Government itself, the more so that no one knew or understood their spirit. From every side they suffered almost incessant persecution; every encounter with a priest, police agent, or magistrate caused them to be brought before the law and imprisoned; every opposition from the neighbouring population was accompanied with dreadful abuse and outrage; their every action rendered them, in the eyes of others, monsters and breakers of the general peace. The higher Government formed its opinion about them principally from the reports of the lower authorities, and they were often sent off into exile as State offenders.

Thus, the persecution of the Spirit-Wrestlers endured until the mild and peaceful reign of Alexander I.[1]

In 1801, the Senators Lopoukine and Neledinski who were sent to examine two of the provinces

---

[1] The persecution of the Spirit-Wrestlers commenced in 1792, when the governor of Ekaterinoslaff reported to Petersburg that "all those infected by this movement merit no mercy"; the sect being represented as particularly dangerous and enticing to adherents, because "the mode of life of the Spirit-Wrestlers is founded on the most honest observances, and their greatest care is the general welfare, and they find salvation in good works." The Spirit-Wrestlers were condemned to be burned, but that sentence was remitted, and they were exiled to Siberia. (Note in the original MS.)

in which the Spirit-Wrestlers lived, were the first to exhibit this people to the Tzar in their true character; and, owing to the report of these examiners, His Majesty, wishing to isolate the Spirit-Wrestlers, graciously allowed them to emigrate to the so-called "Milky-Waters" in the Taurid province.

At the end of the year 1804, the Spirit-Wrestlers living in the provinces of Tamboff and Ekaterinoslaff asked and obtained permission also to be allowed to emigrate to the same place. But before explaining what these people now are, it is necessary to examine their origin, their mode of life, and their teaching.

The Origin of the Spirit-Wrestlers

The name "Spirit-Wrestlers" was given as far back as 1785, probably by the then Bishop of Ekaterinoslaff. It was at the time evidently intended to distinguish, by this name, those holding this teaching, just as the repudiation of ikons (images) was in its time called "Ikon-Wrestling." But the Spirit-Wrestlers themselves, giving their derivation of the name from "spirit," say that they in the spirit strenuously serve God. Thus, following their explanation, the term ought to be understood. The populace called them by various abusive names, such as "milk-men," because they did not fast, but took milk during Lent.

As to themselves, they always called, and call, themselves merely "Christians," whilst others they call "men of the world."

Their origin is unknown, even to themselves; for, being common people and illiterate, they have no written history; neither has tradition preserved amongst them any information upon the subject.

The Society of the Spirit-Wrestlers was originally a dispersed one. Nowhere did they at first form communities, but they lived, a few families in various villages. They were dispersed not only through certain provinces where they were specially strong, but also through almost the whole of Russia. They even affirm that many of their brethren are to be found in Germany and Turkey, but that in Germany they are more severely persecuted than by the Mohammedans.[1]

[1] This calls to our mind a circumstance in the present life of the Spirit-Wrestlers which came to our notice, corroborating the fact that the spirit of the Christian teaching is by nature common to every human being, and that non-Christian peoples are sometimes more sensitive to it than nominal Christians, whose appreciation is so often blunted by too much familiarity with the lifeless letter of the gospel. When the Spirit-Wrestlers were brought into intercourse with the Mohammedan tribes of the Caucasus, these last, awed by the moral purity and elevation of their conduct, came to the conclusion that the Spirit-Wrestlers had in some way got hold of and put into practice the ancient prescriptions of their own Mohammedan faith, which were practically disregarded by the Mohammedans themselves.—(Ed.)

Communication among the Russian Spirit-Wrestlers takes place when occasion offers, for example, when the brethren have to travel upon business; but, when necessary, special messengers are sent.

Their Mode of Life and Organisation

Apart from the question of the peculiarities of their religious faith, the Spirit-Wrestlers may be regarded as affording the model of well-organised family and social peasant life. In 1792, Kohovsky, the governor of Ekaterinoslaff, in his report to the higher authorities, said, amongst other thi_, that the Spirit-Wrestlers are of exemplarily good conduct, and, avoiding drunkenness and idleness, are continually occupied with the welfare of their homes, leading a moral life. They have always regularly paid the State taxes, and fulfilled their other social duties, often even to excess, as compared with the other peasants, owing to the oppression to which they are always subject from the local authorities.

But as soon as question is raised as to principles and actions of theirs which in any way touch their religious faith, there is immediately disclosed a complete difference from, and even opposition to, other peasantry.

The Spirit-Wrestlers never frequent the churches;

they do not worship images; during prayer they do not make the sign of the cross; they do not keep the ordinary fasts, and they take no part in the recreations and loose pleasures of worldly people. There are many such circumstances which completely separate them from all ordinary society of peasants, and which have always been a cause of unceasing persecution against them.

The Spirit-Wrestlers deem that all externalism in the work of salvation is utterly useless, and that the external Church, owing to the lapse of true Christianity, has become a den of robbers; and they therefore acknowledge one sacred, universal and apostolic Church, which the Lord by His coming has assembled, consecrated and replenished by the gifts of the Holy Ghost, and which is, of course, the union of all faithful and true Christians.

In this persuasion, they often have meetings of the brethren; yet they have not for this purpose any specially appointed place, as they do not see any sanctity in locality; but they meet at each other's houses without any distinction. They do not even fix any special days for their meetings, deeming all days equal, and having no holy-days: any free day is a day for their meetings. These meetings, however, in most cases, for convenience' sake, take place during the ordinary Church or national holy-days. Thus, any of them may arrange a meeting at his house by inviting all the brethren. If such a meeting is held at the house of a poor brother who cannot provide food for those who have assembled, then the others previously contribute the necessary food, or else bring it with them; for at these meetings they have supper. Entering the meeting, the men greet the men, the women the women, by grasping each other's right hands, bowing three times and kissing each other. At the commencement, each one says a prayer. The three bows and kisses are intended to signify the cleansing of the body and the repulsion of pride; they take each other's hands as a sign of union and love, kindly expression, good understanding, the sense of a God revered in their souls.

During the meetings, one after another recites the prayers he knows; they together sing psalms and explain to each other the Word of God. As almost all are illiterate, and therefore without books, all this is done from memory. They have no priests in the ordinary sense of the word; they acknowledge as priest the one just, holy, true Christ, uplifted above sinners, higher than the heavens; He is their sole teacher. Thus at their meetings they hear the Word of God from each other; each one may express what he knows or feels for the benefit of his brethren; the women are not excluded from this, for, as they say, women also have understanding, and light is in understanding. They pray either standing or sitting, as the case may be.

At the end of the meeting they again kiss each other thrice as at the beginning, and then the brethren return home.

The virtue most highly respected among the Spirit-Wrestlers is mutual love. They have no personal property; but each regards his property as belonging to all. After emigrating to the Milky-Waters, they proved this in practice; for there they stored up all their property in one place, so that at present they have one common treasury, one common flock or herd, and in each of their villages is a common granary. Each brother takes from the common property that which he needs. Hospitality also is not the least virtue among them, for they take nothing from travellers who stop at their houses, either for lodging or food. However, in order that the brethren may not in time be depraved by casual visitors, they have built in the Milky-Waters a special lodging-house, where such travellers must put up. Here also are received and entertained the Government officials, and here the common treasury is kept.

The Spirit-Wrestlers are compassionate towards their fellow-men. The local authorities themselves, notwithstanding all the calumny they spread against these people, have more than once witnessed before the higher Government to the fact that the Spirit-Wrestlers give help and do acts of great charity to their fellow-men in need. They are compassionate even to household animals, and almost entirely refrain from killing them.

Respect from children to their parents is also strictly observed, and in general from younger men to those older; though the latter, and even parents, do not appropriate to themselves any ascendency over the younger ones, regarding themselves as spiritually their equals.

There exist no punishments among the brethren. As soon as any brother thinks another has behaved improperly, he, according to the precise gospel instruction, reminds him that he is acting wrongly; if the one in fault will not take consideration, he is admonished in the presence of two or three of the brethren; if he does not take heed of them, he is invited to appear before the general assembly.

There have been cases, though very seldom, in which some of the brethren have left the Society, doubtless in order to live at liberty according to their own unrestricted desire. It has even sometimes happened that wives have deserted their husbands. The husbands, in such cases, do not detain their wives, but give them liberty, at the same time giving them means to live upon as far as possible.

Deserters may, however, be again accepted into the Society if they completely repent and leave their immoral life; of which there have also been examples.

The general round of occupations is filled by each taking a calling. Thus the tradesman does the commercial business, and the agriculturist works on the land. But the majority of them are agriculturists, as they give preference to this noble occupation.

In their Society there are no elders who rule or administrate, but rule and administration are by all and each. Written regulations or rules they also have none, and one might suppose that there ought therefore to be disagreement and disorder amongst them. Yet no such disorder has ever been noticed. In the Milky-Waters, three, and even five families, live peacefully together in one large cottage.

As to the management of the families separately, the weakness and dependence of the female sex, the inexperience of youth, and the education of the children, naturally require another system. In every family there must of necessity be an elder one, and the father in the flesh is this elder one.

His duty is to care for the needs of his family, to watch the conduct of the children, correct their faults, and teach them the law of God. When the father dies, his place is taken by the elder of the brothers; and in the case of incapacity of the latter, his place is taken by the one most capable.

The system of education among the Spirit-Wrestlers is most simple and uniform. As soon as the child begins to speak and understand, his parents commence verbally to teach him prayers and psalms, and to tell him something out of the Holy Writings; and they thus continue to instruct him in the Christian doctrine. When the children have learnt a few prayers and psalms they accompany the elders to the meetings, recite in their turn the prayers they have learnt, and sing psalms together with the others. Not only the parents, but every Spirit-Wrestler regards it as his duty to teach every child something useful whenever he has the opportunity to do so, and to keep him from evil whenever he has occasion.

Owing to such education, the spirit of the parents by degrees passes into the children; their ways of thinking take deep root, and the tendency towards good is most strongly encouraged by good examples. It is said, and indeed seems quite natural, that amongst a number of children, one can distinguish

Spirit-Wrestlers' children from the rest, like ears of corn among oats.

Their Teaching.

1. The chief article in the Spirit-Wrestlers' profession of faith is the service and worship of God in the spirit and in the truth.

2. They know no creed, and only say of themselves that they are of the faith of Jesus. The creed which is recognised in our Church, they accept as true in everything, but they regard it as one of the ordinary psalms.

3. They acknowledge God as being in three personifications of the One and Unutterable. They believe that through the *memory* we assimilate ourselves with God the Father, through the *understanding* with God the Son, through the *will* with God the Holy Ghost; also that the first person of the Trinity is the *light*—the Lord our Father; the second person is the *life*—the Son our Lord; and the third person is *peace*—the Holy Spirit our God.

4. The conception they have of Christ is based on the teaching of the gospel: they acknowledge His coming in the flesh, His works, teaching, and suffering; but chiefly they accept all this in the spiritual sense, and affirm that all contained in the

gospel should be accomplished in ourselves. Thus Christ must in us be begotten, born, grow up, teach, suffer, die, revive and ascend; and it is thus that they understand the process of the new birth, or renovation of man. They say that Jesus Himself was and is the Gospel eternal and living, and has sent it forth, preached in the Word. He Himself is the Word, and can be written only on our hearts.

5. They believe that, except through God and His Christ, there is no salvation; but if God is invoked without a pure heart, He Himself cannot save man.

6. For the salvation of man, indubitable faith in Christ is necessary; but faith without works is dead, as also are works without faith. The only living faith is the hearty acceptance of the gospel.

7. Concerning baptism, they say that they are baptized into the Word through the Father, Son and Holy Spirit, as Christ taught the apostles, saying: Go forth and teach all nations, baptizing them in the name of the Father, Son and Holy Spirit. This baptism takes place when a man repents with a pure and willing heart, and calls upon God, and then his sins are remitted, and he turns to God, and not to the world. This is the only baptism for the remission of sins which they profess.

The new birth and baptism, according to their

understanding, are one and the same. The means of attaining the new birth are living faith in God and prayer. The signs of the newly born, or baptized, are the works of the new man.

The consummation of baptism or new birth, they say, a man attains when he is united to God; and such a man may see God with his spiritual eyes. External baptism they regard as useless, saying that water only washes off the uncleanness of the external body.

8. They confess their sins in prayer to the heavenly God, good and merciful, who forgives all our sins. If they sin against their brethren, they confess before all, and ask their brethren to forgive them.

To deny one's sins when others remark them, is regarded by the Spirit-Wrestlers as a great wrong. They also condemn the practice of calling oneself a sinner, and making this a kind of boast, a sham meekness, to excuse one from trying to correct one's errors. When a man has fallen he should immediately recover himself, ask God's forgiveness with humbled heart, and with all his might strive not to fall again into a similar sin.

9. As to the Communion, they partake at all times of the sacred, life-giving, eternal sacraments, in the forgiveness of their sins spiritually, through

the inward acceptance of the Word of God, which is Christ; and such a communion, they say, penetrates the understanding of man, as it were, to the marrow of the bones.

The communion of the body and blood of Christ in the form of bread and wine they do not accept; saying that bread and wine enter into the mouth like ordinary food, and are of no avail to the soul.

10. Fasting they regard as a matter not of kind or quality of food, but of abstinence from gluttony and other vices, of purity, meekness and humility of the spirit. Mere outward abstinence from food does not, according to them, yield any good to the soul.

11. They respect the saints, but do not call for their help, saying that they—the saints—have pleased God on their own behalf, and that we must simply imitate them.

They do not, however, indiscriminately count as good all the deeds of the so-called saints; thus they deem that when St. Nicholas, during a Church Council, hit Arius on the cheek, the Word of God had then deserted him.

12. Marriage amongst them is not regarded as a holy sacrament, and is accomplished merely by the mutual consent of the young couple. As, among the Spirit-Wrestlers, no preference is given to wealth or rank, the parents do not at all

interfere in the marriages of their children. There are also no marriage rites or ceremonies; the mere consent of the two, and a promise to live together, suffices.

Abstinence from marriage for the sake of purity is regarded amongst them as a high virtue.

13. The dead they commemorate by good deeds, and in no other way. God Himself, they say, will remember the righteous in His kingdom. Therefore they do not pray for the dead, deeming it useless. The death of a Christian they do not call *death*, but *change*; therefore they do not say "our brother has died," but "our brother has changed."

14. Concerning the state of the righteous in heaven, they say that the kingdom is in man's will, and that heaven is in the soul; that the souls of the righteous are in the hands of God, and, therefore, no torments of hell can touch them. As to the torments of the unrighteous and hell, they believe that unrighteous souls walk in the dark, expecting soon to perish, and that hell consists in evil feeling.

As to the transformation of souls after death, they believe that man is either justified by deeds, or by deeds is condemned; that the deeds of each man take him to his true place, and that after death there is no repentance.

15. As to the general resurrection of the

righteous and unrighteous, the Spirit-Wrestlers do not enter into discussion, leaving this in the care of God.

16. For a man to save his soul, they do not think it necessary for him to belong to their Society. They say that conduct brings a man salvation, and that for this it is only necessary to understand the way of God, and to follow it.

17. The Spirit-Wrestlers are careful as to the neatness of their houses, and say that for a Christian it is proper to live cleanly and tidily (in this they have always been distinguished from the other peasants in the same village), and that it is only necessary to take care that the spirit be not set upon these things.

They think in the same way about pictures in their rooms, portraits of remarkable men, and even of saints. They say that such pictures serve to ornament the house, and are pleasant for the eye; but they should in no case be worshipped, for that is a deadly sin.

18. The Spirit-Wrestlers like to express their religious thoughts and feelings in the form of allegories. Thus, for example, they speak of seven heavens, the first being humility; the second, understanding; the third, abstinence; the fourth, brotherly love; the fifth, compassion; the sixth, good counsel; the seventh, love, where God lives.

In a similar way they denote twelve Christian virtues, under the guise of twelve friends, thus—

1. *Truth*: which delivers man from death.
2. *Purity*: which brings man to God.
3. *Love*: where love is, there God is also.
4. *Labour*: honourable for the body and helpful for the soul.
5. *Obedience*: a quick way to salvation.
6. *Not judging*: salvation without labour.
7. *Reasonableness*: the highest of virtues.
8. *Mercy*: of which Satan himself is afraid.
9. *Self-Control*: the work of Christ our God Himself.
10. *Prayer and fasting*: unite man with God.
11. *Repentance*: there is no higher law or commandment.
12. *Thanksgiving*: gladsome to God and His higher angels.

We will give, as examples, two of the prayers which are recited at the Spirit-Wrestlers' meetings—

I

To whom shall I go from Thee, my God; from Thy face to whom shall I run? If I were to ascend to heaven, Thou art there; if I descend into hell, Thou art there; if I had wings to fly to the farthest seas, there would Thy arm reach me, and Thy right hand hold me. To whom shall I go, and where shall I find eternal life, if it be not in Thee, my Creator? To whom shall I go, and where, to find consolation, joy, a home, peace for my soul? To whom shall I go from Thee, my Lord God, for Thou hast in Thee the words of life? Thou art the source of life, the giver of all blessings. My soul is thirsting after Thee, my heart is thirsting after Thee, the God of my life! Let us rejoice in Thy sacred name, O Lord Jesus, full of blessing; let my soul be pierced by it, let my heart be penetrated by it, so that nothing in all my life be dearer to me than Thy sacred Spirit. Let Thy words be sweeter to me than honey, let Thy ways of salvation be dearer to me than gold.

II

How shouldst Thou be loved, O God? For Thou art my life, Thou art my salvation, glory, and praise; for Thou art my wealth, my eternal treasure; for Thou art my hope and my trust; for Thou art my joy, my eternal peace. Is it better for me to love emptiness, or the unknown, or that which is perverse, perishable, or untrue, more than Thee, my true life? Thou art my life, my salvation; and therefore in Thee alone do I place all my hope, my faith, my desire. To Thee, Lord, will I call with all my heart, all my soul, all my thoughts; deep into Thee shall I penetrate; to Thee alone shall I pour forth my soul; I shall wholly be in Thee, and Thou in me. I shall see and know in Thee the true and only Lord God, Jesus Christ, whom Thou hast sent. In Thy light shall we see light, by the grace of Thy Holy Spirit.

The Spirit-Wrestlers who, at the end of the year 1804, came to St. Petersburg to ask permission for their brethren to emigrate to the Milky-Waters, when they were leaving Petersburg just before Christmas, were asked whether it would not be better for them to pass the festival in Petersburg, and after that, undertake the journey. They answered: "It is all the same to us, because the festival is in us, within ourselves."

And when, on settling in the Milky-Waters, they were enjoined to live quietly and modestly, and not to endeavour to bring others into their sect, they answered that all that was needed had been already sown; they need no more trouble about that, for now the time was come for the harvest, not the sowing.

[Such is the account given of the Spirit-Wrestlers at the beginning of this century.]

III

THE CHARACTER AND PRINCIPLES OF THE SPIRIT-WRESTLERS TO-DAY

WE have seen what the belief and practice of the Spirit-Wrestlers were a hundred years ago. The vitality and validity of their belief and life are shown by the fact that both survive to this day. The following extract from a letter from one of them speaks for itself as to the spirit in which they live and endure persecution:—

"January 2nd, 1896.

"The concern of most importance to me when thinking of my fellows is, that they might as far as possible try to become humble and meek, which is indispensable for entering the kingdom of God.

"I think that when they have begun to be worried, and their material state to be ruined, they must be very careful not to be tempted. I hold that anxiety for material well-being constitutes already a great stumbling-block and injury to the soul. . . . I ask that you will advise all who know me not to be angry, not to grumble at the Government because it oppresses them. But let them bear, with God's help, any trial which befalls them. Let them only remember what Christ, and afterwards the apostles, had to suffer for the truth. It is important to bear, without complaint, scorn for the truth, but it is still more important, when suffering for truth's sake, to bear that patiently.

"PETER VERIGIN."[1]

A brief sketch of the foundation principles of the Spirit-Wrestlers written by one of themselves is here subjoined:—

"Our brethren are called 'Christians of the Universal Brotherhood' because all men are equal, children of one Father, God; and those who l.ve in deeds and not only in word may belong to it and be members of this universal body. To belong to this Community one has to prove in practice one's love for one's fellow-man, and so a man is able to adopt the essence of Christ's teaching without any external forms or rites. Our brethren having recently adopted this name, try to justify it in practice, and thus to help the human race to adopt the teaching of the Saviour who was, and is still persecuted. Sometimes weakness overcomes us, but this is only the result of habitual evil tendency which shuts out heaven, and there is no more dangerous thing can happen than that. But with God's help there will be men who will conquer their passions and carnal desires, and will serve the living and true God.

"The rules of life of the 'Christians of the Universal Brotherhood' and its general views (at least some of them) are as follows:—

"1. The members of the community revere and love God as the Source of all being.

---

[1] This same Peter Verigin, from his place of exile, wrote a letter to the Empress Alexandra Feodorovna, which is given in the Appendix. He there asks the Empress to intercede in favour of his persecuted brethren for whom he desires permission to emigrate.—(Ed.)

"2. They respect the dignity of man both in themselves and in their fellow-men.

"3. The members of the Community regard everything that exists with love and admiration, and they try to bring up their children in the same tendency.

"4. By the word 'God' they understand,—the power of love, the power of life which is the Source of all that exists.

"5. Life is progress and everything tends towards perfection, in order that the seed received should be returned to the Source of life in the form of ripe fruit.

"6. In everything that exists in our world we see consecutive stages towards perfection,—thus, beginning with a stone and passing over to plants, we come to animals, the fullest development of which is man, regarding him from the point of view of life and of a conscious being.

"7. The members of the Community hold that to destroy or hurt any living thing is blameworthy. In every separate being there is life and hence God, especially in a human being. To deprive a man of life is in no way permissible.

"8. The members accord full freedom to the life of man, and therefore all organisation founded on violence they regard as unlawful.

"9. The basis of man's existence is the power of thought—reason.

"10. It is recognised that the communal life of man is based on the moral law, which has for its rule, 'What I do not wish for myself, that I must not wish for anyone else.'

"These ten clauses we hold to be the fundamental rules of Christian life, or the ten commandments of the 'New Testament.'

"*December 12th,* 1896."

A friend in Tiflis, who has watched carefully the progress of events during the last persecution, thus describes the first impressions made upon him by his intercourse with Spirit-Wrestlers:—

"TIFLIS, *November 17th*, 1895.

"I learned that about twenty Spirit-Wrestlers had come to Tiflis for a few days. I was glad of this opportunity for making their acquaintance. Moreover, I wished to acquaint them with the newspaper article describing the persecutions to which they were subjected during the summer of the last year.[1]

"Having made my way to the inn where they were staying, I found them dining in a small poorly-furnished room. They sat round a simple table, dressed uniformly in long blue coats. Their food consisted of boiled eggs, bread, and grapes.

"After dinner they rose from their seats, and in a low voice offered up a prayer, the words of which I was unable to distinguish. When they learned the purpose of my visit, they were very glad to hear the contents of the article concerning them; they gathered round me and listened with great attention, interrupting me only now and then with exclamations: 'Quite true,' 'This is just what did take place.' After the reading I told them that the article had been published in an English newspaper, and that Leo Tolstoy had also written an article about them. Then I told what I knew of other cases of refusal of military service. They were very anxious to know whether refusals of military service take place also in other countries. Seeing in me a man who sympathised with them, they behaved towards me very cordially, and we parted as friends, sincerely bidding each other good-speed. I had no other opportunity of meeting them, as they returned home early the next morning. They

---

[1] This is an article written by P. Birukoff, who was the first of our friends to go down to the Caucasus, in order to visit the persecuted Spirit-Wrestlers. His correspondence on the subject, accompanied by an introductory letter by Leo Tolstoy, was inserted in the *Times*, October 23rd, 1895, and followed up by an article by Leo Tolstoy in the *Contemporary Review* for November in the same year.—(Ed.)

made a very good impression upon me by their real Christian views and candid, honest and strong characters.

"But a specially strong impression was made upon me by those who have been imprisoned for the refusal of military service. Thanks to an acquaintance of mine, I succeeded not only in gaining admission into the prison, but also in conversing with the imprisoned Spirit-Wrestlers, although unfortunately in the presence of two soldiers, who attentively listened to our conversation. However, I was able to inform them of the above-mentioned article, though there was no possibility of handing it over for them to read.

"I went to these prisoners hoping to encourage them by the information that their noble Christian acts did not remain unknown, and that their example is bound to call forth many followers. And indeed this caused them much joy, but they had no need at all of encouragement; on the contrary, they greatly encouraged me, strengthening in me the wish for a moral Christian life. Instead of unhappy men, I found spiritually healthy and vigorous men awaiting future tortures with gladness. 'It is not for robbery or murder that we are here,' they said to me, 'and therefore one must not grieve at it, but rejoice; Christ Himself suffered.' When I was told that two of them were sentenced to the penal battalion, I could not help exclaiming that it would be hard there. 'We do not care for our flesh, and no one can take away from us our soul,' was their answer, which was uttered in a tone of deep conviction, clearly showing me the sublimity of these true Christians of modern times.

"I felt (myself) as if I had been brought back to the first centuries of Christianity, to the times of persecution of Christians by heathens. Before me stood men who, like the early Christian martyrs, were ready to go to the stake and to suffer any other tortures with joy, ready for any sufferings for the cause of the Christian teaching which they profess. How inferior seemed to me our whole cultured life in comparison with the deep faith and unshaken strength of will of these simple and candid men.

"It is a great sin, said they to me, to lift up one's hand

against one's fellow-man. It is a great pity to kill even a very small bird. Why should we care for our flesh? To-day I am alive and to-morrow I am dead, but my soul is eternally alive; is it not better, then, to let our bodies be injured and to preserve our eternal soul?

"Then the conversation turned to a case which happened not long ago, when a soldier, although recognising the sin of military service, could not make up his mind to refuse it, being afraid to break the oath. This oath, said they, is of no importance. What value has it, if it is taken under compulsion?

"They complained of nothing, but that was certainly because of their convictions. In reality their prison-life is very painful. Their food consists only of bread and water; they are not allowed to write letters freely, and those which are addressed to them go through the censorship of the prison authorities. They are allowed to read only the Gospels and the Old Testament, and this gives them much joy."

In this connection may be given the account received from a military officer, of perfect reliability, who sympathises with the Spirit-Wrestlers, dated 7th March 1897:—

"Having heard that some of the Spirit-Wrestlers were being transferred from the Elisavetpol prison to that of Nukhin, I went out to meet them at the posting station. I shall never forget the look of this 'étape.' Along the high road, muddy with the melting snow, moved a crowd of well-grown, hale people, in so-called 'clean' clothes. They were going along as they pleased with their sacks and cloaks slung soldier-fashion over their shoulders, and but for the escort of soldiers with rifles which surrounded this group of people, and the four natives in irons walking in front (I remembered the words about Christ, 'He was numbered with the transgressors'), one might have fancied they were free travellers.

Their faces were calm and good-tempered, their movements measured, their voices resonant, and their conversation peaceful.

"There were thirty-six of them in all, for the most part middle-aged, though some were quite old and grey, and others quite young beardless lads. The expanse of steppe and fields which for a long time they had not set eyes on, the bright sunshine, the open air, and the sight of other men and of 'free life' evidently had a cheering effect on the captives. The stifling city prison was forgotten for the moment, and each was glad merely to breathe fully and freely, to stretch his cramped limbs, to enjoy the new scene, with no longer around him the walls of the prison court.

"It was just this that made my heart contract painfully as I looked at them. Among them was John Verigin, the father of a young Spirit-Wrestler whom I knew well, and oldest brother of Peter Verigin. He was a tall, handsome old man, very attractive by reason of his intelligence, judgment, and communicative disposition. At my request his companions called him, and we began a conversation, like old friends of long date. Others joined us, and amongst them I recognised a handsome young fellow, who was particularly glad to see me. He had come from Slavianka with a companion to accompany the brotherhood to its destination, and help them to settle down.

"Talking thus, we reached the station, Haldan, where there was a fair that day. The people stared at the new-comers in astonishment and consternation as they approached the 'étape,' for all the people in that part of the world know the Spirit-Wrestlers well. They kept asking each other in an audible tone, 'Why are they taking such people to prison?' 'What have they done?' 'What is their crime?'

"While the party was resting, and the carts with their belongings being reloaded, I spent more than an hour talking with them, standing in the midst of the crowd, and this still more increased the general astonishment.

"The soldiers of the escort apparently behaved in a very friendly manner to the sectaries, and seemed to keep their post at the side of the road merely for form's sake. The sergeant of the detachment had got up a religious discussion, so my friends told me, trying to prove that God had sanctioned and even sanctified war, in proof of which he pointed to the 'Soldier's Pocket Book' of General Dragomiroff, in which we are reminded that there is 'no greater love than this, that a man lay down his life for his friends,' and was greatly astonished to learn that this was somewhat more than a free interpretation of the words of the Bible.

"I went another stage with the convoy and spent the night at the station where it halted. The talk of the Spirit-Wrestlers was of things gone by, of the last persecutions and acts of violence, but chiefly of people in whom they took interest and who shared their religious views. Having accompanied them along the valley half-way through the next stage, I took leave of them and returned home pensive and sorrowful."

The following are conversations related by prisoners in Tiflis which took place between them and the authorities:—

They were asked—

"What are you?"

"We are Christians."

"What sort of Christians?"

"Do you not know what Christians are? A Christian is one who believes in Christ Jesus and fulfils the commandments of God."

"Whose subjects are you? The Turkish Sultan's or the Emperor of Russia's?"

"As a matter of form we pay tribute to the Czar of Russia, but we are the subjects of Jesus Christ."

"And on whose land do you live?"

"We live on God's earth."

"And whom do you obey?"

"We obey Him on whose land we live."

"As you live on God's earth and obey Him, I suppose you do not acknowledge the Emperor?"

"We do not take the Emperor's title from him; as he has been emperor in the past, so let him be in the future. But God created the earth and all that live on the earth."

"Then as you do not refuse to recognise the Emperor, why do you renounce your duties as soldiers?"

"It is not in our power to serve as soldiers, because we are Christians, and a Christian ought not to do violence to his enemies, but to give full liberty to every living being, and not to kill his brother."

"Where did you get this from? Did someone teach you so?"

"We got it from the commandments of God, for the Sixth Commandment says, 'Thou shalt not kill.'"

"And who wants you to kill anybody?"

"How can you say that no one wants us to kill anybody, when you teach the soldier how to kill? We who are Christians cannot kill anybody under any circumstances, because we consider a man the living temple of God."

"Oh yes, it is sinful to kill a man without cause; but what harm is there in killing him in war, when the enemy is coming to plunder us? We are bound to defend ourselves against our enemies, so that they may not plunder us."

"Yes, it is true it is necessary to defend ourselves against our enemies, that the enemy may not be able to enter into a man, and implant evil in him. But we believe that God is our defence and our protector."

"Well, you trust in God, but we will put you in prison, and then we shall see whether God will save you. That is what you get for taking such nonsense into your head as to refuse to serve the Emperor. You might have lived peacefully but for that."

"Why, that is all we wanted, to live peaceably, but it is you who have begun to oppress and compel us."

"Who is oppressing you? You have brought your discomfort on yourselves. Your fathers served the Emperor, but you refuse to do so."

"How can we serve him when he teaches men to kill, and we as Christians are not allowed under any circumstances to kill a man?

We consider it wicked. To us all men are brothers."

"What sort of brother is a man to you when he wants to plunder you?"

"We are not allowed to judge a man. We have one Judge, who is able to save or to condemn us; who are we to judge another? We look on all those who live on the earth according to the word of the Lord, as children of one Father, and our brothers."

"So then you decline to obey the Emperor under any circumstances?"

"We will obey him only in what is not contrary to the will of God."

In conversation with another official, they were asked:—

"What sort of a brother is a man to me when he wants to kill me?"

They answered with another question—

"In what way do you regard the people whom you fight with?"

"We look on them as enemies," the official replied

"And what are you to them?" they asked.

"Why, we are enemies to them," he answered.

"Well, brother, you say that both parties become mutually enemies. Why should you consider yourself an enemy? Would it not be better to look on yourself as the son of the Almighty Creator?"

"Well, of course, everyone would wish to be a son of the Almighty Creator, but it is necessary to deserve it."

"But if you serve God, you will win His approbation. And if you serve man, you will receive approbation from man. Now the applause of man is fatal; it is impossible to serve two masters."

This answer made him very angry, and he retorted—

"I will pull out a revolver, and put a bullet in your forehead, and then you will argue with me no longer."

"Well, if you have the power, kill me. It is written in the teaching, it is impossible to do anything unless God wills it; we cannot make one hair black or white. And we ought not to kill or destroy anything."

"It is so written," he said, "but there is scarcely one of us who can fulfil it."

"How can you say that, when we take such pleasure in endeavouring to fulfil the commandment of God, while you will not let us do so, and do not want to fulfil it yourself?"

"Yes, brothers," he replied, "that is the way of God, but few choose to walk in it, though you, when you have once entered on it, stick fast to it. May God help you to hold fast to it, and not let you wander from it. But mind you don't talk my soldiers over to think as you do."

The men who record these conversations were imprisoned first of all at Kars, for giving back their cards of enlistment, and then they were removed to Tiflis.

We will close this section with an extract from a letter from Gregory Verigin, another brother of Peter Verigin, imprisoned in the Tiflis Metekh Castle—the severest civil place of detention in the Caucasus:—

"I have been told that recently a good many friends and mothers have come to see our brethren in this prison, but to my great regret I could not see them. However, one cannot recall the past—may the will of the Lord be done. I was at the time sitting in solitary confinement in a dark and cold cell in which I passed four days in great suffering. But this is of no consequence, and may be for the best, as it is a good discipline, otherwise man forgets his position on earth; but when he has to undergo such sufferings it reminds him of the eternal life.

"They did not give me any hot food, but I myself decided to pass the time in prayer and fasting. The room was a very small one, and I was given no covering, and had to suffer from cold. When I asked them for a bit of old blanket they alluded to some law or other, and said that this law did not allow it. I told them, 'I am dying from cold and you are talking to me about a law; give me first a blanket, and to-morrow we will discuss the law.' But they shut the door and went away. Oh, hard-hearted men! may God forgive them!"

IV

MILITARY PRISONERS LEBEDEFF AND COMPANIONS

As has been stated, the recent persecutions of Spirit-Wrestlers commenced in 1895, immediately on the revival among them of ancient principles and practice.

The first to suffer were Matthew Lebedeff and eleven other soldiers, who had given way after the universal conscription in 1887, and for a time outwardly submitted to enter the military service. When conviction wrought upon them, and they openly renounced the position into which they had reluctantly, in time of weakness, been dragged, the persecution which fell upon them was more severe than that which came upon those who were called out for the first time.

They were judged by court-martial, and condemned to confinement in the Ekaterinograd penal battalion, where, according to the regulations, they were expected every day and hour to comply with the demands of military discipline, whereas not having accepted the military service they could not with a clear conscience conform to this. On the other hand, the prison authorities had not the right to desist from enforcing these demands; and the consequence was that the Spirit-Wrestlers were subjected to an incessant series of punishments, consisting of flogging, confinement in a cold, dark cell on a diet of bread and water, prolongation of their sentence, etc., which converted their imprisonment into a slow martyrdom,—until, in the autumn of '96, there was issued an order from the Government that those who refused the military service upon religious grounds were not to be imprisoned in military places of detention.

We find in letters many allusions to them and the sufferings they have passed through in the battalion. One Spirit-Wrestler from Signak writes, 4th March 1896—

"They are so wasted in body that one can hardly recognise them."

Others from the district of Gory write—

"We visited Lebedeff and comrades who are in the Ekaterinograd penal battalion; beside these there are eleven other men who have been enlisted recently. We saw them by permission of the colonel, who asked us, 'Where are you from, and what did you come here for?' We answered, 'We came from the province of Tiflis to visit our brethren.' He said, 'Only relatives are allowed to see the prisoners, and that only for a short time, not more than an hour.' And the meeting was under restraint, but still, thank God, we were able to know about their cruel and unmerciful punishments. Their persecutors cut thorny rods, five or six in one bundle. The men were laid down, and on each side of them were placed drunken men, who began to flay them like ferocious wild beasts which tear asunder meek gentle sheep. Each received thirty strokes.[1] After this they were placed in a solitary and cold cell for a day, and the next day they were taken out and guns were given to them, and they were led out for drill. They said, like Christians, 'We cannot fulfil what is against God's commandment.' But, in spite of their answer, they were again beaten and abused. After this drilling came dinner-time for all the prisoners; other prisoners were fed well, but our brethren did not receive even sufficient bread, and yet they were asked, 'Are you satisfied, or do you wish more?' They, in their innocence, said, 'Give us more bread.' But they received instead—blows, such blows that they could hardly stand on their feet."[2]

These tortures were repeated several times and under great physical exhaustion. Of the twelve, three had not the power to remain steadfast. The fortitude they manifested at the beginning of their imprisonment temporarily gave way, and when guns were given to them, they consented to hold them—also, while faint and weak they took meat

---

[1] Others write: "The blood splattered in all directions; the prickles entered into the flesh, and when they were pulled out, bits of flesh fell down."

[2] Being vegetarians they could not take the soup which was given to the other prisoners.—(Ed.)

LEBEDEFF AND COMPANIONS

which was contrary to their principles. For this they sorely reproached themselves, the more so because when some of their brethren in prison with them were transferred from the prison to Siberia, these three who thus gave way in weakness were left behind and treated as soldiers. They still remain in the Ekaterinograd penal battalion. They feel their position keenly, but endure with patience, though very weak and ill, and manifest much tenderness of spirit. A visit paid to them in December '96 is thus described by a correspondent :—

"*January* 1897.

"Anthony Fofanoff from Elisavetpol went to see the brethren who were left behind in the penal battalion— Matthew Lebedeff, Nicholas Fofanoff, and Kalmikoff. He went there on the 25th December 1896. He visited them, and talked with Lebedeff, who, in reply to Anthony's question, why he stayed there in that murderous place, said that he had been the object of a severe attack on the part of the authorities.

"His story was as follows :—'They sent letters addressed to me from the brethren, the purport of which was to beg me to fortify the brethren who were in the battalion. The colonel was furious with me, and had me repeatedly flogged for it, for such letters always pass through his hands.'

"He begged me to give this message to all the brethren and his mother. :—

"'Please God, I shall recover. My heart is very sore that I could not hold out against the whole of the punishment'; and again, 'I shall get over it, I am very grieved myself about it.'

"When Anthony gave them bread and provisions, Lebedeff

was much touched, and exclaimed, with tears in his eyes, 'I thought you had forgotten all about us, and that we had forfeited your affection by our want of fortitude.'"

Previous to this, in November 1896, Leo Tolstoy wrote a letter to the colonel of the penal battalion, and near the same time V. Tchertkoff also wrote to him.[1] These letters appear to have somewhat softened the heart of the colonel, to judge by the following account from a friend in Tiflis:—

"TIFLIS, *December* 1896.
"An old Spirit-Wrestler, Tcheveldayeff, has just returned to Tiflis from the Ekaterinograd penal battalion. He had gone to visit his son for the second time. The first time he had been there in the spring of 1895. The commander of the battalion had a little time before received letters from some friends of ours which acquainted him with the real nature of the Spirit-Wrestlers' teaching, with the reason why they were punished, and which asked him to treat them as kindly as possible. This is what Tcheveldayeff related to me about his interview with the commander :—
"Upon receiving me the commander said, 'Ah, old man ! you came in spring, and now here you are again !'
"'Yes,' said I, 'I have come again ; I feel for my children.'
"'Why do you say your children? You have only one son here, have you not?'
"'Yes, but I regard them all as my children.'
"When I was there in spring he was hard-hearted, but this time he was much kinder. I used to go and see him every day, and when I did not come he sent a soldier for me. We used to sit down on a bench outside his house and chat.

---

[1] Both these letters are given in the Appendix.—(Ed.)

"'Now, if they were to submit themselves to our law, I should let them go home to see their friends,' says he.

"'One should serve one Master only,' says I.

"'And what master?'

"'We have one Master—the Lord—Him do we serve.'

"'Why did you not accept the guns?'

"'How can we kill our friends?'

"'And an enemy?'

"'If one were to kill an enemy, one would become an enemy oneself. The Lord has created all in the same image.'

"'But if someone were to meet you and take your horse?'

"'I would earnestly ask him not to take it. But if I should not persuade him; then let him take it. I will not take sin upon me. As I was coming here with a young friend of mine, we met an Ocetin [one of the native tribes of the Caucasus] who untied my cape and took it; we prayed him earnestly to return it. He did not, but rode away with it. He will be uneasy. The cape will cause his soul much trouble.'

"The commander asked me, 'What is this command of yours, "Love thy neighbour as thyself"? You have no books, where then did you find it?'

"'We received it from our Father and Friend. It is in our "Book of Life," which contains all our commandments.'

"He made me repeat them to him. Then he asked me to repeat to him one of our psalms.

"'Where do you learn all this?' he asked.

"'From our parents.'

"'And thus you teach your children?'

"'Yes.'

"And so we went on chatting together. At last he said, 'Yes, all this is correct; and one should live so.'"

Of those Spirit-Wrestlers who were transferred from the penal battalion and other prisons to Siberia, several became ill and died, from the hardships they endured in prison and on the way. The following is a short account, from a friend of ours, of one of them who died in the Moscow prison:—

"At the present moment there lies in the Moscow Prison Hospital a Spirit-Wrestler, one of the recalcitrant soldiers. He was in confinement about a year, and was deported with others to the Yakutsk district, but left behind at Moscow owing to illness. I have been to see him twice. He has consumption, and looks very bad, and will not long hold out against the fever, the perspirations, and the cough. In mind he is quite at rest, and says he is satisfied with everything, and only complains of his disease, though he bears even that with complete equanimity.

"*March* 1897."

V

THE BURNING OF ARMS, JUNE 1895, AND "THE EXECUTION"

WE must now turn to what occurred in June 1895, when the Spirit-Wrestlers, by common agreement, went to the place appointed near the village of Goreloe, carrying the arms which were to be committed to the flames. (It needs to be clearly understood that these arms were not the property of Government or landlords, but simply the few weapons they, like the surrounding natives, had been accustomed to keep for self-defence against robbers, wild tribes of hillsmen, and wild animals; they now became conscious that even to keep these weapons in their houses was a yielding to weakness, and contrary to their principles.) Without inquiry or waiting for evidence, the Cossacks were quickly called out to suppress what was falsely reported to be a rebellion, and very violent was their attack upon the inoffensive people.

While these Spirit-Wrestlers were being driven away to the village of Bogdanovka to appear before the Governor of Tiflis, this is what they sang:—

"For the sake of Thee, Lord, I loved the narrow gate;
I left the material life; I left father and mother;
I left brother and sister; I left my whole race and tribe;
I bear hardness and persecution; I bear scorn and slander;
I am hungry and thirsty; I am walking naked;
For the sake of Thee, Lord."

And the Cossacks tried to drown their voices with obscene songs. Then these Cossacks were quartered on the villagers, who received much rough treatment from them.

Helen Nakashidsy of Tiflis,[1] who from the first has been in warm sympathy with the Spirit-Wrestlers, and who is now in England, thus describes what she was told of the cruelty practised:—

"*July* 1895.

"I heard the following account from Akcenia Strelaeva, a woman no longer young:—

"'Four of us—women—were going from Spaski to Bogdanovka On the road we were overtaken by a hundred Cossacks, who brought us into Bogdanovka. They there placed us in a coach-

---

[1] By birth Princess, which title, however, her present convictions do not allow her to accept.—(Ed.)

house, and then led us out one by one into the yard. Then they stripped us in the yard (throwing our skirts over our shoulders), and flogged our bare bodies. In the yard stood some Cossacks and many other people. There were only a few of our own people. They flogged us so, you could not count the strokes; two of them held us and four flogged! Three of us stood through it, but one they dragged about so that she could not stand. We received many insults.'

"Nastasia Tchornenkova, a very aged woman, spoke as follows:—

"'A whole platoon and two sotnias [1] of Cossacks lived in our yard at Bogdanovka. They lived in the coach-house. One night we sat down to supper—I, my husband, our two sons (one nineteen, the other seventeen years old), and our daughter-in-law, who had been confined only fifteen days before. The Cossacks came up. "You are having supper?" they asked.—"Yes, sit down and join us."—"The commander has ordered us to arrest the master of the family."—"If you arrest him, you must take us as well." Then they began to drag the master along; we clung to him and would not let go; and, my God, what happened! We cried out, "Help, brothers!—who believes in

[1] Sotnia—a detachment of Cossacks, corresponding to about a squadron. Sotnik—commander of a sotnia.—(Ed).

God, help!" They dragged us in this manner round the yard—they dragging the master and we clinging to him; then they tore him away from us, and locked him in the storehouse. There they beat him so, they scarcely left him alive. The shrieks were dreadful!

"'They locked me in the hut, and left my daughter-in-law in the yard I escaped from the hut through the window, and a neighbour hid me. They took my daughter-in-law into a room and tortured her for three hours. They abused her, and said, "Where is your God? He will not save you." The sotnik came, and would also have abused her, but when she said to him, "I shall remain alive, thou shalt perish; I shall die, thou shalt perish," he rushed out into the yard, and then back into the hut. Then he again wished to abuse her; thought she would yield and be submissive, but she said the same thing to him "I shall remain alive, thou shalt perish; I shall die, thou shalt perish." At last the sotnik ordered the Cossacks to retire, as she did not yield to them.

"'In the morning they let the master go, and we went to him and wept. He also wept, and said, "What shall we do? Let us pray to God; we have done no wrong, have robbed no one, have not disgraced ourselves."'

"She told me this weeping all the time—the old women were all bathed in tears; there were in all fifteen men there, and they wept likewise.

"'Then,' she continued, 'they went into the village. They went to Thena Saprikina's, where she was with an old man and her daughter, and abused them in the same way.

"'Then they abused Tania Posniakova. Her husband was not at home, but her cousin was spending the night there. They locked him in the stable.

"'It was just the same at Mitro Malakhoff's— they locked him up, and abused his wife to their heart's content.'

"And this is what Anna Posniakoff, a very old woman, told me:—

"'They [the Cossacks] came to us during the day—twenty of them. They called my son, Vassia, twenty-four years old, into the yard, and set him to sweep up the rubbish into a small bag. He made signs with his hands and stood back. They brought a whip to him. Then they seized him and put him in the coach-house. When it was growing dusk, they brought him out into the yard, and flogged him as much as they wished. After they had flogged him three times, they raised him up; he breathed, so they went on again. When they stopped he was barely alive, his whole body

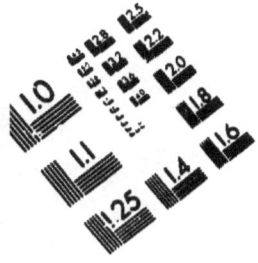
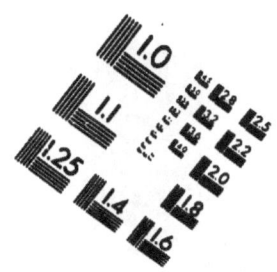

**IMAGE EVALUATION
TEST TARGET (MT-3)**

Photographic
Sciences

23 WEST MAIN STREET
WEBSTER, N.Y. 14580
(716) 872-4503

hacked. They then flung him into the coach-house.

"'At midnight they came to arrest another son. We said, "We are all the same; arrest us all! We will not let him go alone." Two of the women had little children whom they took up in their arms, the little ones clinging tightly to them; they almost stifled the children trying to tear us from them. They dragged him along, and us with him. Then the Cossacks got frightened for the children, and tried to tear us away. They went into the coach-house where my son was whom they had flogged; there they kindled a light, and then all approached us. "Spare me, an old woman," I cried; "take whatever you like, but do not insult us; I am really like a mother to you all." Then one of them came and asked them not to alarm us. They took us into a room where the sergeant-major was lying on a bed. We all fell on our knees before him. "May God pardon you for tormenting us so," we cried. They then turned us out of the village, and in the morning we got up and went away. All our property was gone, and there was no one to whom we could go. In three days we returned, to find empty boxes and nothing in the house.

"'They also flogged Vassia Kolesnikoff. They flogged him so that his boots got full of blood.

They did not flog anyone else, but there was scarcely a man whom they did not beat.'

"Nicholas Posniakoff said:—

"'They [the Cossacks] came running to my place one night. They yell, "Open!" I reply, "We have no lodgings for the night." Then they began knocking at the door. I found some way of hiding my two daughters in the hut, and ran myself into the coach-house by secret doors. They dragged the mistress and the little one off the stove on to the ground. When she cried, "Piotka [her sixteen-year-old son, who happened to be there], knock at the window; Nicholas is in the yard, and will come and help us," they threw her down and ran out. There was no further violation of the women, but they beat them dreadfully.'"

This is what Posniakoff sang three times while he was being flogged:—

"Lord, my Saviour, Thou art my light! whom shall I fear? The Lord Himself watches over my life; of whom shall I be afraid? Though they bring my flesh to harm, my enemies shall be put to shame. Let mine enemies rise up against me, yet will I not fear this; though a host should rise up against me, my trust is in the Lord. My father and my mother deserted me in my infancy. My Saviour took me up, and gave me life and prosperity. Place me, O Lord, in the way of truth by Thy holy law. Let not mine enemy trouble me! I trust in the life to come, but do not leave me in this life, O Lord, to the hands of the ungodly. Cover me, O Lord, with Thy right arm from all lying slanderers. Let my head now be lifted up against all terrible enemies. I offer with my heart a sacrifice. I call upon Thee, O Lord, in the psalms of those that serve Thee. With my heart and soul I cling to Thee; let me in truth not be confounded, for my trust is in God! To our God be glory!"

VI

CONSCRIPTION, ARRESTS, IMPRISONMENTS, EXILE

FROM this time a long history of arrest, imprisonment and banishment begins. A friend before alluded to in Tiflis writes :—

"From the accounts of the Spirit-Wrestlers, among other things, this very characteristic fact becomes clear : the military authorities have no desire whatever to listen to their explanations as to the causes of their refusal to engage in military service, and they even peremptorily prohibit them from talking about it. The Spirit-Wrestlers of the 'Great Party' were summoned to the recruiting offices in the following places, in Suram, Dushet, and Signak, and everywhere they finally refused to draw the lots, although every one of them appeared at the recruiting stations.

. . . .

"The General Surovtzeff, in conversation with them, said, 'You do not fulfil the law of the Emperor'; they answered, 'As for this law, we are only told about it, but for some reason or other we do not see it. What is the use of a law if it can be bought? Here is the chief of the Kars district, Shegoubatoff, who took a thousand roubles from a man, who applied for a certificate, excusing his son from military service.' And Shegoubatoff himself was present, and stood there turning quite pale, but did not utter a single word, because it was true, and the man who gave the thousand roubles was also there."

The following is from a letter from the Spirit-Wrestlers in the Elisavetpol prison :—

"*November 29th*, 1895.

" Dear brother in the Spirit,—We greet thee, and in the name of our Lord God and Saviour Jesus Christ wish thee to have life and health, and send thee a low salutation.

"We have for some time heard about our brethren living in different parts of the Russian State. Not knowing where they live, it is difficult for us to have earnest mutual intercourse with them, which brings consolation in our earthly life, and helps in gaining the knowledge of the way to eternal salvation.

"Now, dear brother,'we desire to make thy closer acquaintance. We have seen thy letter of Nov. 11th, in which thou askest one of our brethren concerning the life of the banished Spirit-Wrestlers in the Caucasus. Concerning this we will tell thee, dear brother, that when we lived according to our own fleshly lusts, and served our own pleasure and lived in compliance to those around us, then the Caucasian officials liked us; especially when we gave to every government official in our towns every kind of bribe. They then called us a well-meaning people, and said that there was no people better than the Spirit-Wrestlers. But when the Spirit-Wrestlers began to accomplish the will of God and to serve the only Lord, at the same time ceasing to give bribes, the officials immediately changed their opinion about us, and now say, 'You are criminals against the Emperor.' But if the Emperor knew who are the real criminals against the law, he would put them under a special judgment."

Here is a letter from a Spirit-Wrestler from the district of Kars :—

IMPRISONMENTS, EXILE 67

"On the 15th November 1895 there was a conscription by casting lots. Our young men refused to take part in it. One of the officials drew lots for them; the lot fell to five of them, whereas in all there were thirty-two of ours. The others had to take tickets for the reserve, but they refused. They were all put in prison.

"Two days previously, there came to us a general and a colonel in order to ascertain why the Spirit-Wrestlers refuse the military service. Four elders from each village were called to the house where these officials put up.

"The officials asked: 'How is it that the Spirit-Wrestlers, who formerly lived quietly and were in repute all over the Russian Empire for their good life, at the present time have grieved the higher authorities by refusing to acknowledge any authority?'

"Then they asked, 'Why do you not accept the military service?'

"It was answered them: 'We cannot kill nor use violence, according to the Word of God, towards our brothers who are created in the image of the Lord.'

"'But how is it you did not know this formerly?'

"'Formerly we also well knew the Lord's law, but did not profess it, living disorderly and giving way to drunkenness.'

"Then they said, 'Perhaps here you are oppressed, or the land is not good? If you were transferred on to good land, would you accept the military service?'

"'We cannot leave the law of the Lord.'

"Then they said, 'Well, you will be banished to Siberia, and there you will suffer every kind of misery.'

"'Whatever is done to us, we cannot leave the law of the Lord and fulfil the law of man.'

"Then they said, 'We will restore to you your houses and the common treasury you formerly possessed; will you then serve?'

"It was answered them, 'We cannot desert our Lord.'"

And again, this is from a letter from some

Spirit-Wrestlers while on their way under escort to prison from Kars to Tiflis :—

"*December* 1st, 1895.

"Dear brother in the Lord Jesus Christ and kind sister,—

"We testify to you that, according to the grace of our Lord God, we are in health and welfare. Glory to Him for His care and guidance over us. And you, dear brother and sister, are you in health and welfare?

"To-day we have received a letter from J. Tregouboff, in which he greets us with brotherly good wishes and salutation, the Lord save him! He writes that he has 'heard that I and Verestchagin are condemned to be hanged, and that he and V. Tchertkoff have written to the Commander-in-Chief of the Caucasus, asking for a remand. I do not know how such a rumour reached them; as yet we have not heard anything about it. Perhaps, indeed, this is being perpetrated against us. This evil is their affair. Our business is to fulfil the work of the Lord, who has given us life and light. We are of course thankful to these our brethren, that they from the overflow of love in their hearts are caring about us, the Lord save them: but according to our understanding it is not proper for a Christian to bow his neck before men and ask for mercy. We for such deeds expect mercy from the Lord, who is merciful to, and saves His people when they truly serve Him in His law, and we wish to attain the honour of being His servants.'

"He further writes: 'The teaching of your brethren is near to us. Can you send us an account of your faith?' I would be glad to write a letter, but while travelling under escort you yourself know how difficult it is. In connection with the work we have begun, I think that not much verbal explanation is necessary. In what our faith consists, I may briefly say: in two commandments brought us by the Saviour of the world, as to loving Him, and loving our neighbour as ourselves.

"We took leave of our parents when on our way, and also of the brethren and sisters who accompanied us some distance,

IMPRISONMENTS, EXILE   69

with a feeling of brotherly love, and who with joy cried to God asking Him to give us the welfare of firmly standing on the word of God, and of conquering the spirit of evil by patience.

"On the 14th, General Surovtzeff and Colonel Grebenstchikoff, both from Tiflis, visited the village of Spasovka, in the district of Kars. Four of the brethren from each village were called, and questioned as to how it was they had in so short a time changed their mode of life. They answered all the questions with reason in a Christian way. May the Lord Jesus Christ send peace and grace into their hearts that they may live according to His covenant."

Our friend in Tiflis writes with regard to the recruiting:—

"It is evident the military authorities did all in their power to conceal, not only the causes of the opposition [to military service], but even the very existence of such refusal. [Men who had been distributed among the detachments were not even compelled to take the oath, nor led out to drill.] And the local papers are prohibited from printing any articles whatsoever on the Spirit-Wrestlers. But 'the light shines even in darkness, and the darkness cannot conceal it,' and there is nothing in secret which will not become known, and therefore all the endeavour to hide the truth came to nothing, and only proved that the persecutors themselves at the bottom of their soul do not hold themselves right, although they feign to look upon the persecuted with contempt."

With regard to the Commission alluded to in one of the foregoing letters, the same friend writes:—

"The Commission has been constituted exclusively of military men; but one must do it justice by saying that one investigation was done thoroughly, and the information was collected carefully. This Commission went round the whole district inhabited by the Spirit-Wrestlers of the 'Small' as well as of the 'Great Party.'

"First of all, the Commission arrived in Signak, where the Spirit-Wrestlers were summoned from the neighbouring Georgian settlements. They appeared at once, according to the invitation, and were treated very civilly. It is said, for instance, that first of all they were asked to sit down, and were even told they are looked upon as brethren (though I think such behaviour of the military class doubtful). But this is certain, that the chairman of the Commission said to them, 'I ask you to tell the whole truth quite freely, because we are sent by the Emperor to learn the whole truth.'

"From Signak the Commission went to the village of Slavianka in the province of Elisavetpol, thence to the villages of Kirilovka, Terpayne, and others in the province of Kars, then to villages in the district of Ahalkalak, and everywhere made circumstantial inquiries, especially about the 'execution.'

"As to the violation of young girls, they did not at first wish to believe the facts, and sought out the victims, who affirmed them. One of the latter who was examined became angry, and said to them, 'Why do you torment me? For the fourth time you are asking me the same questions. I tell you the truth, why then do you annoy me further?' Generally speaking, the Spirit-Wrestlers of the 'Great Party' told the Commission everything. One of them said to the general, 'You wish to compel us to fulfil the laws, but you yourselves commit iniquities.' The general answered nothing, but afterwards he remarked to the colonel, who stood near him, 'That Spirit-Wrestler was right.'

"Generally the Spirit-Wrestlers assert that they are ready to obey kind and just authorities, *i.e.* when the claims of the authority do not contradict the law of God. But certainly they cannot obey the authorities unconditionally. In regard to this they point out Christ's words that one 'cannot serve two masters.' One of the Spirit-Wrestlers jokingly remarked that some of their well-wishers are probably not pleased because they (the Spirit-Wrestlers) do not clean the boots of the officials. In this was expressed the fact that the Spirit-Wrestlers of the 'Great Party' behave themselves towards any authority with marked independence, which naturally does not give satisfaction. Holding all men to be brethren, they do not recognise any difference in the social position of men. The Spirit-Wrestler will not, like the orthodox peasant, stand at the door of a so-called gentleman, bowing low, but will freely shake hands and sit down, side by side, unconcerned with any surroundings, or the title, rank, or position of his companion, which behaviour naturally grates upon the officials. Moreover, the Spirit-Wrestlers speak candidly, and are not afraid to tell men the truth to their face, which is especially displeasing to those who are used to conventional lies."

The same writer continues his account:—

"TIFLIS, *January 18th*, 1896.

"The Spirit-Wrestlers who have recently visited me informed me of new persecutions which have been taking place quite lately. It had seemed as though one might expect a change for the better towards the Spirit-Wrestlers, but by the information I have received I am terrified, and convinced that the struggle of 'darkness against light' is raging with new force.

"Now, imagine, in the province of Kars during December 27th, 28th, and 29th of last year there were many arrests in the villages of Kirilovka, Spasovka, Terpayne, and Gorelovka, and one hundred men of those arrested were sent to the military prison of Kars. Then on January 8th fifty-seven Spirit-Wrestlers of Kars were removed from the Kars military prison to the prison castle of Tiflis behind the Metekh prison, on the outskirt of the city, and no one is admitted to see these prisoners.

"Following them came their relatives, who, during the winter frosts, crossed the mountain ridges to visit the prisoners, to say to them a word of comfort, and perhaps to part with them for life. But they were driven away from the prison, and were not allowed even to have a glance at the unhappy prisoners, who are shut up in such a way that it is quite unknown how they are dealt with there.

"Not long ago letters have been received from Spirit-Wrestlers, who, after refusing military service, were sent to the penal battalions in the province of Tersk. They write that they are treated most cruelly; they are beaten and starved, not receiving even sufficient bread, and at the same time compelled to do work beyond their strength. Evidently every kind of ferocity of the authorities against the Spirit-Wrestlers is growing more and more. It is indeed said that Shervashidze [the governor of Tiflis] prepared for his own justification a pamphlet about them, and I believe that, wishing to clear himself, he did not spare the colours in denouncing the Spirit-Wrestlers persecuted by him."

"TIFLIS, *June 20th*, 1896.

"Concerning the material wants of the Spirit-Wrestlers I have learned the following : In the district of Signak they almost starve from hunger, there is no bread at all ; in the district of Gory there is a little, but many people die here and suffer from sickness on account of the change of climate. Their food consists of bread only. They have received bread from the province of Elisavetpol, and money from Kars. During the winter they received from the Spirit-Wrestlers of Kars more than 10,000 roubles. They need help—and that considerably. One of the Spirit-Wrestlers of Kars told me yesterday that they [*i.e.* the Spirit-Wrestlers of Kars] intend to help them, and that they are collecting accurate information concerning their needs.[1] All this information will be sent also to you.

"Not long ago a Spirit-Wrestler, Barabanoff, died in the Metekh prison from rapid consumption. He was buried by

---

[1] They did help to the utmost of their ability, and now these resources are exhausted.—(Ed.)

the brethren, and on the tombstone the following epitaph was engraved: 'Eternal memory to the Christian D. T. B., who by God's will died in chains for truth!'"

The prisoners in Elisavetpol received a visit from a missionary of the Synod, with regard to which one of them writes :—

"V. Skvortsoff has not visited us much, and when he came his conversation was about the Emperor. He said that as a priest is responsible for the sins of his parishioners, so is the sovereign for the sins of the soldiers. Then he added that we must defend our fatherland from foes; but we answered to this that our fatherland is in heaven, and we are pilgrims on the earth. And he said, 'But if a horde of Turks came to conquer you, what would you do then?' We answered, 'It is all the same to us; we are all created in the same image.' He said, 'Is the Turk also created after the image of God?' He said it deridingly, and added, 'It will be difficult for you to suffer so heroically.' He is of middle size, with a little blackish beard, and seems to be thirty-five or forty years old. In conversation he is very cunning and quick. He visited at Kars and the province of Tiflis, among the settlers, and questioned them all."

A detailed letter about other conversations with Skvortsoff was taken away from V. Tchertkoff by the authorities, together with many other valuable papers, when his house was ransacked by the police, previous to his exile.

The following are some more letters from Spirit-Wrestlers.

From the Spirit-Wrestlers in the Elisavetpol prison :—

"*June 8th*, 1896.

"Dear friend and brother in Christ Jesus,—We inform thee that, according to the mercy and grace of our God and Lord Jesus Christ, we are all in peace and welfare. We heartily greet thee and thy brethren, and wish you welfare in your lives. May God sustain thee, dear brother.

"Though we are strictly watched in order that we might not be in communication with you and the other brethren, yet we cannot be silent.

"When we lived in the flesh, according to our lusts, we conformed to the ways of the world, we were the slaves of sin, we pleased the carnal man which leads into pride and perdition of pride, through the love of money and lust, through fornication, intoxication, superstition, murder, and the shedding of the blood of one's brothers; when we broke the law of God and His commandments, when we lived according to the world,—then we were loved and called good men; but when we turned away from the ways of the world, when we began to fulfil the law of God, the commandments of Jesus Christ and of our conscience,—then we became hated, slandered, and put into prison on the pretext that we do not accept the power of the Emperor.

"Dear brother, can the power of man have authority over men when it cannot make one hair white or black, and, contrary to the will of God and the teaching of Jesus Christ, compels people to take oaths and fulfil the military service,—when it teaches to kill, to sustain bloody wars, and to call one's brethren foes and enemies? What a great mistake this is! Are we not all the children of the same Father? . . . He is the King of all kings and the Lord of lords. His reign is without beginning and without end. . . . But men have turned away from the works of God, have forgotten the God who sustains them, have followed the flesh according to their lusts, have 'loved darkness rather than light because their deeds were evil.' They have hated each other, the father has turned against his son, and the son against his father; they bring their own brethren before the judgment of men; they put people into prisons and penal battalions and torture them for their refusal to accept the military service, and for their knowledge of the truth. A true Christian cannot make war and shed the blood of his brother, but, on the contrary, he loves him more than himself; for this our brethren are dispersed in painful and distant exile, in order to prevent the spreading of the knowledge of the truth and of the teaching of Jesus Christ, which is contrary to the ways of the world, to 'Babylon and her adultery.'

"Dear brother, one looks at such rulers and on their unmerciful actions, and one wonders how it is they are not conscious of the higher power of the Lord over them. Every living creature calls forth unto the Lord expecting a speedy deliverance; especially do the sons of God expect redemption from the slavery of the son of sin. Let us ask God to give us patience in meekness to endure these persecutions, calumny, insult, blows, humiliations, suffering and illness, for this will obtain the love of God.

"Dear friend, they know not what they do. They think that by such unreasonable, self-w... unmerciful tortures they please God. Forgive us, Lord... s... 'nners and our persecutors! Turn them away, Lord, ... the way of iniquity, and teach them the way of truth! May the Lord God hear the groans, wailing, and cries, the voice of prayer of His servants; may He liberate from servitude His people and save them from the nets thrown over them! The net will be dissolved, then the sinners will cry and wail on account of their wrong deeds, and the righteous will rejoice in the salvation of their souls in the kingdom of God."

From Spirit-Wrestlers in the Elisavetpol prison, in response to a greeting from some members of the Society of Friends :—

"*May* 7th, 1896.

"Dear brother and friend in the faith of Jesus Christ, the merciful Saviour of the world,—Thy letter of April 6 and the extracts from the English letters we have received, for which we thank thee much. God save thee for thy earnest and simple-hearted love. We also thank the English brethren in the faith of Jesus Christ. The Lord save them with His eternal salvation for their faith in God the Father and Son and Holy Ghost. Dear brother, we ask thee, if possible, to transmit from us our sincere and hearty feeling of love, with entire good wishes to the brethren who are in England ; may God send them health and steadfastness in faith.

"Portions of our correspondence with thee have fallen into the hands of the authorities. The colonel of the gendarmes has read them to us, and we are deprived of freedom in answering thee; they are now strictly watching our correspondence.

"Be of good cheer and strong in the Spirit! May the Lord liberate all who live on the earth from servitude.

"THY BROTHERS," etc.

We will close this section with a striking illustration of how conviction works sometimes in the minds of the authorities, when they are confronted with the faithful testimony and clear reasoning of the Spirit-Wrestlers, and the great difficulty they have in knowing how to deal with them. The friend who writes the following letter took down the history of the conversation from the lips of an eye-witness, "a young man who had already served his time as a soldier, sprightly, enterprising and clever."

"To the conscription of the year 1895, in the district town of Dushet, there were summoned seven of the Spirit-Wrestlers who were exiled to the Gory district. They were all entitled to exemption owing to their domestic circumstances. They obeyed the summons, but declined to draw lots, and

IMPRISONMENTS, EXILE

the village alderman was told to draw for them. A report was drawn up of their refusal, and they were sent home again. The judge determined that they were to appear before the Court on the 14th of November, and served them with notices to do so on the spot.

"They appeared at the Court at nine a.m. The judge said, 'Are you the men who refused to draw lots?'

"'We are.'

"'And why do you refuse?'

"Glagolieff: 'Because we do not wish to enter the military service, knowing beforehand that such service is against our conscience, and we prefer to live according to our conscience, and not in opposition to it. Although by the military law we are entitled to exemption, we would not draw lots because we did not wish to have any share in a business which is contrary to the will of God and to our conscience.'

"The Judge: 'The term of service is now short: you can soon get it over and go home again. Then they will not drag you from court to court, and from prison to prison.'

"Glagolieff: 'Mr. Judge, we do not value our bodies. The only thing of importance to us is that our conscience should be clear. We cannot act contrary to the will of God. And it is no light matter to be a soldier, and to kill a man directly you are told. God has once for all impressed on the heart of each man, "Thou shalt not kill." A Christian will not only not learn how to kill, but will never allow one of God's creatures to be beaten.'

"Then said the judge, 'But, nevertheless, we cannot do without soldiers and war, because both you and others have a little property, and some people are quite rich; and if we had no armies and no soldiers, then evil men would come, and thieves, and would plunder us, and with no army we could not defend ourselves.'

"Then Glagolieff replied, 'You know, Mr. Judge, that it is written in the Gospels, "Lay not up to yourselves treasure upon earth." We have obeyed this injunction, and will hold to it, and therefore shall have no need of defending anything. Why, ask yourself, Mr. Judge, how we can keep our money when our brothers need it? We are commanded to help our neighbours, so that we cannot find rest in our souls when we see them in want. Christ when He was on earth taught that we should "feed the hungry, give shoes to those who have none, and share with those who are needy."'

"Then the judge began to inquire into our circumstances, and asked how we were getting on, and how the country suited us, all about the distraint, and the Cossacks striking the women and old men, and their outraging the young women, and expressed great astonishment that soldiers, whose duty it was to protect us, could turn themselves into brigands and murderers.

"Then said Glagolieff, 'We see from this, Mr. Judge, that an army does not in the least exist for the protection of our interests, but in order that our savings may be spent on armaments, and is no use in the world, but to cause misery, outrage, and murder.'

"Then the judge, who had listened to it all attentively, was greatly moved and distressed by all the cruelties which had been practised on the Spirit-Wrestlers. He condemned them, in virtue of some section or other of the Code, to a fine of three roubles, and himself advised them not to pay it.

"He talked a great deal more to us, and questioned us, and said, as he dismissed us, 'Hold fast to that commandment of the Lord's.'

"We went to the inn to dine, and see our friends, and before we had had any dinner, the judge came to see us, and brought us two roubles, in case we had nothing to eat. We endeavoured to decline the money, saying, 'We do not want it. Thank God, to-day we shall have enough.' But he begged us to accept it as the offering of a pure heart, and made in sincerity, and then we took it, as from a brother, and after thanking him, and bidding him farewell, went away. He showed us where he lived, expressed a wish to know more of us, and begged us to come and talk with him."

VII

PRESENT CONDITION OF THOSE WHO WERE BANISHED, ETC.

So much for the history of some of the prisoners. Those who were banished have not fared much better. Out of sixteen villages (containing in all about 1886 men), 287 adults and 112 children, visited this year, were found to be suffering from hemeralopia, or hen-blindness [1]; 113 adults and 40 children were suffering from other eye diseases, and a few were quite blind; 57 adults and 31 children suffered from dysentery; 86 adults and 22 children were seriously ill. Almost the whole population suffered more or less from fever. Their earnings are very small, in some villages nothing at all, and yet in most places they have rents to pay. But the picture is by no means entirely a dark one. Notwithstanding the fact that such an increase of population must be a considerable burden upon an already poverty-stricken district, there are many

[1] See note, p. 81.

indications that the Spirit-Wrestlers are winning the respect and love of those among whom they are settled. As early as 6th February 1896 one of them wrote:—

"Some Molokans [a Russian Evangelical peasant sect] have begun to afford help to people; they bring bread and money to the prisons. Glory be to God! And some of the natives have begun to consider our conduct and many of them approve it, and thank the Lord God for it."

And on 28th December 1895 our friend in Tiflis wrote:—

"Recently I have heard that the ideas of the Spirit-Wrestlers have begun to spread among the Georgians in the villages where the Spirit-Wrestlers have been settled. It is said that the Georgians were impressed by the fact that the Spirit-Wrestlers, in spite of their own great poverty, began to help them with their work. They sometimes even gave away to the poor Georgians the wages which they received from the landlords."

On the other hand, they have often been very roughly treated, especially by officials. The same writer says, 24th January 1896:—

"From the Spirit-Wrestlers who are settled in the Georgian villages come sad news of the continuous oppressions on the part of the authorities, and of iniquitous impositions, because these authorities, availing themselves of the fact that the Spirit-Wrestlers are recognised as criminals, do not think it necessary to be ceremonious towards them, and draw off from their bodies the last shirt, take away the last bit of bread, and only the strongly-developed sense of mutual help among the Spirit-Wrestlers preserves them from complete destitution."

The following letters (one from a friend who visited them before he himself was banished to Courland, and the other from a friendly local landowner) further describe the present state of affairs amongst them :—

[From J. Tregouboff, at the present time in exile at Goldingen in Courland, Russia, about 12th April 1897.]

"I have seen the sufferers in the three districts of Tionet, Gory, and Doushet. They were all very glad to see me, and asked me to transmit their greetings to all their brethren.

"There are the most cases of illness in the Gory district, and, I hear, in that of Signak. Almost all suffer from hen-blindness,[1] and they become so accustomed to it that they do not regard it as a disease. But they are also suffering from another most dreadful eye disease ; their eyes at first become red and are very painful, then they become covered with a white film, and at last quite blind. Such cases are numerous, and are becoming more and more so.

"I saw one girl who was all the time sitting with her face covered. When I approached her and asked her to lift her handkerchief, I saw a white face and white (very slightly

---

[1] This term is used in Russia to indicate a state of periodical blindness which comes on daily towards sunset, and is in Russia one of the most frequent effects of insufficiency of suitable nourishment.—(Ed.)

greyish) moving eyes, and I was startled,—it was as if I saw a statue. She does not see objects. The film had been removed at Tiflis, and she began to distinguish light from darkness, but she cannot distinguish objects. Another girl whom I saw has one eye already white and blind and the other red. She also sits continually. I was also told about a boy whose eyes got covered with a white film and then burst and ran out.[1]

"Besides this dreadful and strange disease they are exceedingly exhausted by fever, dyspepsia, cough, pain in the legs, swelling of the legs and other parts of the body. In one village I found a prostrate invalid in almost every habitation; other invalids could stand on their feet. Many of them die. They subsist on bread and a little quantity of salted cabbage.[2] Many prepare for themselves a soup made from kvas[3] and horse-radish. A very few make their soup of millet, cheap rice, or buck wheat.

"As you know, on the 10th December they decided to sell a part of their horses and carts, and they left themselves from two to three horses and one cart for every twenty men, as they will have to emigrate to the place of their permanent establishment when the Government has decided that question. The money obtained by this sale, together with that which was in the hands of private members of their community and offered by them to the common treasury, composed at the end of 1896 a capital of 15,000 roubles.[4] Of these, 9000 are already spent, and the other 6000 will not, according to their calculation, last for more than two months longer.[5] For every man (including also the expense upon the horses) about two roubles[6]

---

[1] We have information from various sources that there are many precisely similar cases.—(Ed.)

[2] This kind of cabbage is commonly used by the peasants with their food.

[3] A common Russian beverage.

[4] About £1500.

[5] This fund is now completely exhausted.—(Ed.)

[6] About 4s.

OF THOSE WHO WERE BANISHED 83

a month are necessary. As in some places (namely, in the Gory and Doushet districts) small earnings are obtainable, they do not quite spend the two roubles per man. At all events, for two months they will have some food, though insufficient and unsuitable.

"Their further fate they commend into the hands of God, and are ready to suffer all."

A local landowner of the Gory district, upon whose estate upwards of thirty families of exiled Spirit-Wrestlers have been established, has given the following information concerning these Spirit-Wrestlers and those who are living in the neighbourhood :—

"At first the sufferers were in a dreadful condition; they had to live in little huts, about thirty men in each; the absence of fuel, the want of food, and close atmosphere told upon them most severely; about half of them then died out. The native peasants, Georgians, at first did not pay any attention to them, and the rougher ones oppressed them—stole their horses and other property; but when the natives found out that the Spirit-Wrestlers established amongst them live according to the gospel, do not resist evil, but willingly give all they have to those in need, and to those who take it from them with violence, they themselves began to protect them from unkind men, and now help them in every way they can, regarding them as righteous men.

"At first when the Spirit-Wrestlers had just settled down, the natives used their labour almost gratuitously, and it was well if their most strenuous exertions, altogether unfamiliar to the natives, were paid for by a piece of bread. The Spirit-Wrestlers did not complain, and were satisfied with that which was given them. At the present time the natives endeavour to surpass each other in affording earnings to the Spirit-Wrestlers.

"As at first, so also now, the district overseers, following the orders of the local lay and clerical authorities, do not allow the Spirit-Wrestlers to bury their dead, neither in the cemeteries nor in anyone's land. There have been, for instance, cases where the Spirit-Wrestlers, while travelling to the places of their exile, have, many of them, died on the way from hunger and illness, and those who survived were obliged to take the corpses along with them, as they were nowhere allowed to dig graves for their interment. At present the natives, both nobles and peasants, ask the Spirit-Wrestlers to bury their dead in their private gardens, which neither the local administrative nor the clerical authorities are able to forbid.

"In general the native Georgians, having come to know the Spirit-Wrestlers, do not know why these righteous people are being exterminated, are indignant against the authorities, and are doing their best to help and protect the sufferers, though this 'best' is more valuable spiritually than materially, for it is so little they can do, owing to their own poverty and subjection."

One typical case of starvation and suffering may be given—

"Avdotia Dubinkin, a widow, exiled to the district of Gory, and living there with five children, and her brother-in-law and his wife with four children, lost in the course of one year four children, while four more fell seriously ill; the brother-in-law and his wife died. H. N."

There is not space to tell all that one would. We have a letter from John Sherstobetieff (a Spirit-Wrestler) telling how some members of the "Small Party" side with the authorities in oppressing the others. Also how Government officials distrain for debt, taking away clothes, etc., far in excess of the amounts owing.

On 6th May an exile from the Signak district wrote :—

"Not long ago I was in Tiflis, and we went to the Commander-in-Chief, Prince Galitzin, on 30th April, expressly to learn about how our affairs, *i.e.* our exile, stood. His answer to us was, 'Your exile is unlimited, because you will obey no one.' We could not refrain from telling him God's truth—that we did obey, only we could not become soldiers."

["On this," says another witness, "he instantly replied, 'That is just what you are suffering for. You have nothing left because you risked all to have your own way. Now you must get your food as best you may.'"]

The letter continues—

"It was plain that he did not want to listen to us.

"There is no work here except mowing, which will last for another month. Materially we are as badly off as ever. Not long ago a friend from Russia came to see us, but he was not allowed to do so, and was sent back at his own expense.

"There are many sick and dying among us, but we will endeavour to approach spiritual perfection. . . .

"I remain your brother in Christ, who loves you from the bottom of his heart,   VASILI POTAPOFF."

The same writer wrote on 10th April :—

"Medicines and doctors may, to our minds, stay where they are. They are difficult to get and cost much money. If it is in your power to give material help, then send us as much as you can, for all of us exiles are in want of the same thing. In all the four districts there are about 6000 roubles to 3500 souls.[1] According to our calculation, 20 persons and 3 horses cost 40 roubles a month. There is most sickness in the Signak district, and some in Gory and Doushet. The complaints are fever, œdema, internal inflammation, and dysentery. There are also bad coughs, and people suffer from their eyes. All the money we have put into one fund, even that which the brethren sent us. In some parts they are working for what they can get—in the Gory district about the railway there is a little work to be had, but nowhere else is there any. The total number who have died in the four districts, that is since our exile in 1895, is 470 persons [which number has considerably increased since April].

"The total number of the living is 3500. I cannot tell how many are sick, but really in the present state of affairs not above one in a hundred is quite well."

One of the last accounts we have from a friend in Tiflis, who says—

"*May 20th*, 1897.

"I cannot report anything of an encouraging nature with regard to the present condition of the Spirit-Wrestlers. They live as before, scattered in different villages; their earnings are extremely small—the great majority earn nothing at all; they sicken and die, but not to the same extent as in winter, which is easily understood, for the vivifying power of spring-time has a beneficial effect on their health.

"Their position of uncertainty binds them hand and foot; they cannot take land on lease from proprietors and sow it so as to have corn and forage for themselves and their horses for winter, for there is risk at any time that they may be driven elsewhere, and all their labour and expense lost.

[Here follows an account of the visit to Golitizin told elsewhere.]

"Evidently the Government desires to keep them in this

---

[1] All spent some time ago.—(Ed.)

OF THOSE WHO WERE BANISHED 87

state of material uncertainty, so that they may be obliged by sheer force of hunger to fall in with the proposals of the Government. But this calculation is erroneous, for the Spirit-Wrestlers stand by their principles with amazing staunchness. 'We will all perish,' say they, 'but will not desert our faith.'

"The money they have in hand amounts only to one thousand five hundred roubles, which will be exhausted in a very short time. Their position has become exceedingly critical. If you can obtain anything in the way of pecuniary help for them, please do so with all speed."

There was a notable trial in the Tiflis District Court on 9th April. A group of Spirit-Wrestlers of Slavianka in the Elisavetpol government were charged with "resistance to the authorities." In reality they had not only offered no resistance to the authorities, but the latter had acted in a revoltingly arbitrary and cruel way towards them, without succeeding in exciting the slightest revolt on the part of the victims. The true circumstances of the case were disclosed very clearly during the trial, but the Court was so biassed by the influence of the local authorities, that, contrary to all evidence, it condemned the Spirit-Wrestlers to severe punishments, thereby arousing the extreme indignation of the public present at the trial.

It is well worth remarking how the spiritual revival before alluded to, which took place among the Spirit-Wrestlers after their disasters suffered from the Government, reacted upon their practical conduct.

In the autumn of 1893, at a general meeting of the elders, they decided to cease using intoxicants, these being liable to lead men into temptation; to cease smoking, and thus avoid luxury; and to cease eating meat, confessing it a great sin to take away the life one cannot give. In this they resumed the practice of their fathers.

Another most important principle which they revived, was the communal ownership of property, thus returning to that practice of the first followers of Jesus, which has been so soon, so entirely, and for so long forgotten by all who call themselves Christian. This remarkably illustrates the simple way in which certain reforms, representing the highest aspirations of the most advanced portions of so-called civilised humanity,—generally so much and so fruitlessly discussed and quarrelled over,—are quietly realised in practice, as the natural result of an inner sense of brotherhood, when this feeling is indeed genuine and has developed in a given body of people, upon a true spiritual basis.

Let us describe how this took place in the words of one of the Spirit-Wrestlers themselves:—

"In the summer of 1894 we liberated ourselves from the evil of the division of property. We called to mind the words of the Lord as to the first commandment being, to 'love God with all one's heart, mind and strength,' and the second one like unto it, to 'love one's neighbour as oneself.' Upon these two commandments stands the law of God. And my spirit wishes to fulfil God's law. That which I do not desire for myself, I do not desire for my brother. We, the elders, therefore, met in the village of Orlovka, worshipped God, and decided to divide all our property equally amongst us. After that, in every village the money owned privately was brought to one place and put into the hands of the local elders. It was not only the poor brethren who agreed to this, but also the rich ones. Tchernenko, for instance, had a fortune of 25,000 roubles [about £2500], and he gave all up. Other rich brethren did the same.

"No moral pressure was brought to bear upon anyone, for it was desired that the sacrifice should only be made voluntarily and with love. If such deeds as these are done with effort and pain of heart, it is better to refrain from them.[1]

"The elders, having collected the money, first of all paid the private debts which were owing, and the rest of the money they divided equally amongst all. Each one received about ten roubles [£1], including women and children. The cattle and all other farming accessories were also equally divided among all; and the hired Armenian labourers were discharged.

"After this, those who came to be in need received what they wanted gratuitously from those who possessed more, without being required to return it.

"We began to plough and mow in common. We would gather together about one hundred and fifty of us, and mow the fields, first here, then there, as rapidly as if they had been burnt by fire. The corn and hay we divided according to the number of consumers in each family. The workshops also became

---

[1] In this case, a certain number of individuals, in various families and villages, amounting, together with the women and children, to about three thousand, not being prepared to participate in this division of property, had the share of the family wealth proportionately due to them settled upon them, and thus formed a third party, who though sympathising with the remaining twelve thousand of the "Great Party" were not ready to go so far as them in their self-renunciation.—(Ed.)

communal: large rooms or barns, full of people, some coming, others going, old men, young ones, boys,—each doing some work or other, necessary for himself or for others, and no question of payment for the work.

"When we began to live in this way we all felt ourselves quite other men, as if we had afresh been born into God's world. Even the most decrepit old men, who formerly could do no work owing to their weakness, even they revived in spirit, and took to working with the rest, if it were only at something unimportant, as, for instance, the twisting of ropes, in order that they might not find themselves alone and inactive."

Since the first division of property, above described, which took place about three years ago, the Spirit-Wrestlers of the "Great Party" have several times repeated the same method, whenever the inequality of property in private hands became sufficiently pronounced. And it is only this remarkable practice of mutual brotherly solicitude, together with the help they have received from outside, which has enabled them to support so effectively those of their brethren who have been utterly ruined and exiled by the Government.

One may say, without exaggeration, that this uncultured and almost illiterate people manifest in all their practical proceedings the most perfect exactitude of organisation; such as might be envied by many of those much more intellectually developed, who nevertheless so often fail in this respect. And indeed this could not be otherwise,

OF THOSE WHO WERE BANISHED 91

for the spirit itself of true Christian relationship is after all the only condition requisite for the attainment of all necessary practical purposes.

So, for instance, in the case of affording material help to the starving exiled brethren. The overseers elected by the Spirit-Wrestlers from amongst themselves, for the purpose of distributing relief, had before them a task exactly opposite to what is usually the case in similar circumstances. Generally such overseers have to take great care that the help distributed should not get into the hands of those less needy but more presumptuous; whereas in this case the overseers have to search for the needy ones, as many of those in the worst condition prefer to remain at home without food for several days rather than apply for help, which they think is as much needed by other brethren as by themselves.

With regard to such true Christian conduct, the life of the Spirit-Wrestlers, under their present condition of spiritual enlightenment and fervour, affords innumerable illustrations, the description of which would in itself form another volume. Such a record would certainly serve as a startling condemnation of the coldness and selfishness of formal Christianity.

VIII

CONCLUSION BY LEO TOLSTOY

THE facts related in this Appeal,[1] composed by three of my friends, have been repeatedly verified, revised, and sifted; the Appeal itself has been several times recast and corrected; everything has been rejected from it which, although true, might seem an exaggeration; so that all that is now stated in this Appeal is the real, indubitable truth, so far as the truth is accessible to men guided only by the religious desire, in this revelation of the truth, to serve God and their neighbour, both the oppressors and the oppressed. But, however striking the facts here related, their importance is determined, not by the facts themselves, but by the way in which they will be regarded by those who learn about them. And I fear that the majority of those who read this Appeal will not understand all its importance.

[1] See Chapter I.

"Why, these fellows are a set of rioters; coarse, illiterate peasants; fanatics who have fallen under evil influence. They are a noxious, anti-governmental sect, which the Government cannot put up with, but evidently must suppress, like every movement injurious to the general welfare. If women and children, innocent people, have to suffer thereby, well, what is to be done?" This is what, with a shrug of the shoulders, people who have not penetrated the importance of this event will say.

On the whole, this phenomenon will, to most people, seem devoid of interest, like every phenomenon whose place is strongly and clearly defined. Smugglers appear — they must be caught; anarchists, terrorists — society must get rid of them; fanatics, self-mutilators — they must be shut up, transported; infringers of public order appear — they must be suppressed. All this seems indisputable, evident, decisive, and therefore uninteresting.

And yet such an attitude towards what is related in this Appeal is a great error.

As in the life of each separate individual (I know this in my own life, and everyone will find similar cases in his own), so also in the life of nations and humanity, events occur which constitute turning-points in their whole existence;

and these events, like the "still small voice" (not the "great and strong wind") in which Elijah heard God, are always not loud, not striking, hardly remarkable; and in one's personal life one always afterwards regrets that at the time one did not know and did not guess the importance of what was taking place. "If I had known it was such an important moment in my life," one afterwards thinks, "I would not have acted thus." It is the same in the life of mankind. A Roman Emperor enters Rome in noisy, pompous triumph—how important this seems; and how insignificant, it then seemed, that a Galilean was preaching a new doctrine, and was executed therefor, just as hundreds of others were executed for similar, as it seemed, crimes. And so now, too, how important, in the eyes of refined members of rival parties of the English, French, and Italian Parliaments, or of the Austrian and German Diets, and in the eyes of all the business men in the city and of the bankers of the whole world, and their press organs, are the questions as to who shall occupy the Bosphorus, who shall seize some patch of land in Africa or Asia, who shall triumph in the question of Bimetallism, and so on; and how, not only unimportant, but even so insignificant that they are not worth speaking about, seem the stories which tell that somewhere in the Caucasus, the Russian Government has taken measures for crushing certain half-savage fanatics, who deny the obligation to submit to the authorities. And yet, in reality, how not merely insignificant, but comic, beside the phenomena of such immense importance as are now taking place in the Caucasus, is the strange anxiety of people, full grown, educated, and illuminated by the teaching of Christ (or at least acquainted with this teaching, and capable of being illuminated by it), as to which country shall have this or that patch of land, and what words were uttered by this or that erring, stumbling mortal, who is merely a production of the surrounding conditions.

Pilate and Herod, indeed, might not understand the importance of that for which the Galilean, who had disturbed their province, was brought before them for judgment; they did not even think it worth while learning wherein consisted his teaching; even had they known it, they might have been excused for thinking that it would disappear (as Gamaliel said); but as for us, we cannot but know the teaching itself, as well as the fact that it has not disappeared in the course of eighteen hundred years, and will not disappear until it is realised. And if we know this, then, notwithstanding the insignificance, illiterateness, and obscurity of the Spirit-Wrestlers, we cannot but see the whole importance of that which is taking place among them. Christ's disciples were just such insignificant, unrefined, unknown people, and other than such the followers of Christ cannot be. Among the Spirit-Wrestlers, or rather, "Christians of the Universal Brotherhood," as they now call themselves, nothing new is taking place, but merely the germinating of that seed which was sown by Christ eighteen hundred years ago, the resurrection of Christ himself.

This resurrection must take place, cannot but take place, and it is impossible to shut one's eyes to the fact that it is taking place, merely because it is occurring without the firing of guns, parade of troops, planting of flags, illuminated fountains, music, electric lights, bell-ringing, and the solemn speeches and the cries of people decorated with gold-lace and ribbons. Only savages judge of the importance of phenomena by the outward splendour with which they are accompanied.

Whether we wish to see this or not, there has now been manifested in the Caucasus, in the life of the "Christians of the Universal Brotherhood," especially since their persecution, a demonstration of that Christian life towards which all that is good and reasonable in the world is striving. For all our State institutions, our Parliaments, societies, sciences, arts,—all this only exists and operates in order to realise that life which all of us, thinking men, see before us as the highest ideal of perfection. And here we have people who have realised this ideal, probably in part, not wholly, but have realised it in a way we did not dream of doing with our complex State institutions. How, then, can we avoid acknowledging the importance of this phenomenon? For that is being realised towards which we are all striving, towards which all our complex activity is leading us.

It is generally said, that such attempts at the realisation of the Christian life have been made more than once already; there have been the Quakers, the Menonites, and others, all of whom have weakened and degenerated into ordinary people, living the general life under the State. And, therefore, it is said such attempts at the realisation of the Christian life are not of importance.

To say so is like saying that the pains of labour which have not yet ended in birth, that the warm rains and the sun-rays which have not as yet brought spring, are of no importance.

What, then, is important for the realisation of the Christian life? It is certainly not by diplomatic negotiations about Abyssinia and Constantinople, papal encyclicals, socialistic congresses, and so on, that mankind will approach to that for which the world endures. For, if the kingdom of God, *i.e.* the kingdom on earth of truth and good, is to be realised, it can be realised only by such attempts as were made by the first disciples of Christ, afterwards by the Paulicians, Albigenses, Quakers, Moravian Brethren, Menonites, all the true Christians of the world, and now by the "Christians of the Universal Brotherhood." The fact that these pains of labour continue and increase does not prove that there will be no birth, but, on the contrary, that the birth is near at hand. People say that this will happen, but not in that way,—in some other way, by books, newspapers, universities, theatres, speeches, meetings, congresses. But even if it be admitted that all these newspapers and books and meetings and universities help to the realisation of the Christian life, yet, after all, the realisation must be accomplished by living men, good men, with a Christian spirit, ready for righteous common life. Therefore, the main condition for the realisation is the existence and gathering together of such people who shall even now realise that towards which we are all striving. And behold, these people exist!

It may be, although I doubt it, that the movement of the "Christian Universal Brotherhood" will also be stamped out, especially if society itself does not understand all the importance of what is taking place, and does not help them with brotherly aid; but that which this movement represents, that which has been expressed in it, will certainly not die, cannot die, and sooner or later will burst forth to the light, will destroy all that is now crushing it, and will take possession of the world. It is only a question of time.

True, there are people, and, unfortunately, there are many, who hope and say, "But not in our time," and therefore strive to arrest the movement. Yet their efforts are useless, and they do not arrest the movement, but by their efforts only destroy in themselves the life which is given them. For life is life, only when it is the carrying out of God's purpose. But, by opposing Him, people deprive themselves of life, and at the same time, neither for one year, nor for one hour, can they delay the accomplishment of God's purpose.

And it is impossible not to see that, with the outward connection now established among all the inhabitants of the earth, with the awakening of the Christian spirit which is now appearing in all corners of the earth, this accomplishment is near at hand. And that obduracy and blindness of the Russian Government, in directing persecution against the "Christians of the Universal Brotherhood," a persecution like those of pagan times, and the wonderful meekness and firmness with which the new Christian martyrs endure these persecutions— all these facts are undoubted signs of the nearness of this accomplishment.

And therefore, having understood all the importance of the event that is taking place, both for the life of the whole of humanity and for the life of each of us, remembering that the opportunity to act, which is now presented us, will never return, let us do that which the merchant in the Gospel parable did, selling all he possessed that he might obtain the priceless pearl; let us disdain all mean, selfish considerations, and let each of us, in whatever position he be, do all which is in his power, in order,—if not to directly help those through whom the work of God is being done, if not to partake in this work,—at least not to be the opponents of the work of God which is being accomplished for our good.

LEO TOLSTOY.

December 14th, 1896.

APPENDIX I

LETTER FROM PETER VERIGIN TO THE EMPRESS ALEXANDRA FEODOROVNA[1]

MAY the Lord God preserve thy soul in this life, as well as in the future age, Sister Alexandra.

I, a servant of the Lord Jesus Christ, am living in the testimony and glad tidings of His truth. I am in exile since the year 1886, from the Spirit-Wrestlers' Community of Trans-Caucassia. The word "Spirit-Wrestler" should be understood thus: that we in the spirit and with our soul profess God (see,—the Gospel; the meeting of Christ with the Samaritan woman at the well).

I implore thee, sister in Christ the Lord, Alexandra, pray thy husband Nicholas to spare the Spirit-Wrestlers in the Caucasus from persecution. It is to thee that I address myself, because I think thy heart is more turned towards the Lord God. And there are at this moment more women and children suffering: hundreds of husbands and parents are confined in prisons, and thousands of families are dispersed in the native villages, where the authorities incite the population to behave coarsely with them. This falls specially heavily upon the Christian women! Lately they have been putting women and children into prisons.

The fault on our part is that we, as far as it is possible to

---

[1] This letter has on two occasions been placed in the hands of Court ladies, who have near access to the person of the Empress, but it is unknown to us whether it was, by them, transmitted to the Empress. —(Ed.)

APPENDIX I

us, endeavour to become Christians. In regard to some of our actions, our understanding may not be sufficiently enlightened.

Thou art probably acquainted with the teaching of vegetarianism; we are sharers in these humanitarian views. Lately we have ceased to use flesh as food,[1] and to drink wine, and have forsaken much of that which leads to a dissipated life, and darkens the light of the human soul. Refusing to kill animals, we in no case regard it as possible to deprive *men* of life. If we were to kill an ordinary man or even a robber, it would seem to us that we had decided to kill Christ.

The State demands that our brethren should learn the use of the gun, in order to know well how to kill. The Christians do not agree to this; they are put into prisons, beaten and starved; the sisters and mothers are coarsely defiled as women, very often with railing exclamations. "Where is your God?" "Why does He not help you?" (Our God is in heaven and on earth and fulfils all His will.)

This is sad especially because it is all taking place in a Christian country. Our community in the Caucasus consists of about twenty thousand men.[2] Is it possible that such a small number could injure the organism of the State, if soldiers were not recruited from among them? At the present moment, they *are* recruited, but uselessly: thirty men are in the Ekaterinograd penal battalion, where the authorities are only tormenting themselves by torturing them.

Man we regard as the temple of the living God, and we can in no case prepare ourselves to kill him, though for this we were to be threatened by death.

---

[1] The Spirit-Wrestlers were vegetarians, at least as far back as the beginning of this century; towards the middle of the century they had relaxed in this respect, as well as in regard to their other principles.—(Ed.)

[2] In this number are also included the five thousand who have betrayed their original principles, and whom we have described as the "Small Party" in Chapter I.—(Ed.)

APPENDIX I

The most convenient manner of dealing with us would be to establish us in one place where we might live and labour in peace. All State obligations in the form of taxes we would pay, only we cannot be soldiers.

If the Government were to find it impossible to consent to this, then let it give us the right of emigration into one of the foreign countries. We would willingly go to England or (which is most convenient) to America, where we have a great number of brothers in the Lord Jesus Christ.

From the fulness of my soul I pray the Lord for the welfare of thy family.—The servant of Christ,

PETER

(living in exile in the Government of Tobolsk).

APPENDIX II

LETTER FROM LEO TOLSTOY TO THE COMMANDER OF THE
EKATERINOGRAD PENAL BATTALION

SIR,—Pardon me, please, for addressing you without using your Christian and parental names. I have not been able to ascertain them; but the matter of enormous importance, as well for me as for you, concerning which I have to write to you, does not bear delay.

This matter concerns the confinement in your battalion of the Caucasian Spirit-Wrestlers who have refused military service.

The military authorities, who have condemned them, and you, who are executing on them the sentence of the Court, evidently regard the conduct of these men as harmful, and believe in the efficacy of those severe measures which are directed against them. But there are people, and many (to whose number I also belong), who regard the conduct of the Spirit-Wrestlers as great heroism, most useful for humanity. In this light, such conduct was regarded by the ancient Christians, and similarly it is, and will be regarded by true Christians of the new time.

Thus the views concerning the conduct of the Spirit-Wrestlers may be entirely opposite. In one point only all are agreed, both those who regard this conduct as good and useful, and those who believe it to be harmful :—on this point, namely, that men who refuse the military sevice from religious conviction, and are ready to endure for this every kind of suffering and even death, are not vicious, but highly moral men, who, owing merely to a misunderstanding of the authorities (a misunderstanding which will probably soon be corrected), are placed in the same position as the most criminal soldiers.

I understand that you cannot take upon yourself to correct the mistake or misunderstanding of the higher authorities, but that while on service you have to fulfil the duties involved. This is certainly so ; but beside the duties of a service which you have voluntarily taken upon yourself, duties obligatory for you only during the small period of your life,—you have, like every man, duties not temporary but eternal, which have been laid upon you independently of your own will, and from which you cannot liberate yourself.

You know who these men are and wherefore they are suffering ; and knowing this, you may, without overstepping the limits of your rights and duties, refrain from leading them into fresh disobedience, and from subjecting them therefore to punishments ; you are in general able to have compassion for them, and as far as possible to alleviate their lot ; as you are also able voluntarily to shut your eyes to the distinction between these men and the other prisoners, and to torture them to death, as has been the case in the Voronege penal battalion with an ex-schoolmaster, Drojin, whose case is now generally well known, he dying a martyr to his Christian convictions.

In the first case, you would receive the gratitude and blessings of the sufferers themselves, of their mothers, fathers, brothers and friends, and above all, you would find in your conscience the incomparable joy of a good deed. In the second case (I do not speak of the prisoners themselves, because I know that they will find consolation in the consciousness that by their death they are confirming their faith), what dreadful accusations against yourself you will arouse by your cruelty, from the parents, relatives and friends of those who may perish under your command ; and above all, you would yourself incur such rebukes of conscience as would not leave you the possibility either of joy or peace.

You could indeed say : " I do not know, and do not wish

to know wherefore these men are sent to me, but since they are sent, they must fulfil the lawful demands etc.," if you really did not know this. But you do know—if it were only through this my letter—that these men are sent to you because they wish to fulfil the law of God, which is equally binding upon you as upon them,—the law of God, which not only forbids us to kill or torture each other, but enjoins us to help and love each other.

And therefore, if you will not do all that is in your power to alleviate the lot of these men, you will bring upon yourself an invisible but most heavy calamity in the consciousness of the evident transgression of the will of God, as known to you; the consciousness of an irreparable, cruel, evil deed.

This is why the case I am writing to you about is of the highest importance and urgency. As for me, the matter is of great importance, because if I did not say all this, I should feel myself in fault before you, before myself and before God.

Everything on earth can be corrected except an ungodly and inhuman action, especially when one knows that it is ungodly and inhuman, and nevertheless commits it.

Pardon me, please, if I have said anything objectionable. Truly, before God, can I say that that which I have written, I have written only because I regarded it as my duty to you to do so.

I should be very grateful to you if you were to answer me.—With respect, I remain, yours sincerely,

LEO TOLSTOY.

November 1st, 1896.

APPENDIX III

FROM VLADIMIR TCHERTKOFF'S LETTER TO THE COMMANDER OF THE EKATERINOGRAD PENAL BATTALION

... From the enclosed pamphlet,[1] if you will read it, you will learn the object of the present letter. Notwithstanding the complete difference of our relations to this question, I think you cannot but agree with the chief considerations contained in this paper.

At the present time there is, in the penal battalion under your command, a whole group of "Spirit-Wrestlers," who, on account of their religious convictions, are unable to take part in military service, and therefore find themselves in this military place of confinement, in an exactly similar position to those individuals concerning whom I have given information in that paper. Even although one were to regard the convictions of these men as erroneous, as you naturally cannot fail to do, yet one cannot but admit that, in connection with their views, they manifest remarkable conscientiousness and true courage, in striving not to deviate from that which they for themselves regard as the will of God, notwithstanding the dreadful sufferings, and in some cases even death, to which they are subjected in consequence. Therefore no honest man, whatever his relation to the military service, can fail to

---

[1] A pamphlet entitled "Unnecessary Cruelty," by V. Tchertkoff, in which the author shows that, even from the point of view of the State, it is neither necessary nor advantageous to make martyrs of those who, owing to their religious convictions, cannot take part in the military service.—(Ed.)

regard, at all events with respect and compassion, these martyrs for conscience' sake, and desire, as far as it lies in his power, to alleviate their sufferings.

I implore you, sir, carefully to investigate the conduct of these men, and to enter into the motive which prompts them to act as they do. If you will only do this, you will immediately see for yourself that they radically differ from all the other prisoners under your command, and that it would therefore be too unjust and cruel to make the same demands upon them as upon the other prisoners, and to submit them to the same punishments for the non-accomplishment of these demands. If an ordinary prisoner evades the fulfilment of the official demands made upon him, he does so in accordance with quite another kind of impulse, having no connection with the demands of conscience; whereas these men are in your battalion, placed in such a position that many of the demands of the authorities, which in the eyes of the other prisoners have nothing objectionable, are for them contrary to the will of God, as they understand it in relation to themselves. And just as no true Christian will regard it as admissible to attempt to convert a heathen from faith in idols to the true God by means of flogging, imprisonment and threats, so also those who do not share the convictions of these men cannot conscientiously regard as admissible the use of compulsory measures with a view to forcing them to act contrary to their faith, before they are inwardly convinced of the falsehood of that faith.

We all know what a dreadful responsibility is incurred, before God, by him who, for whatever purpose, endeavours to force a man to act contrary to his conscience. May God help us to avoid that responsibility. "We all walk under God,"[1] and very soon—much sooner than we generally suppose—will come for each one of us the day of reckoning before Him. And we all know that before that highest tribunal, not human but divine, we have to answer, not

---

[1] A Russian proverb implying that we are all responsible to and dependent on Him.—(Ed.)

for any digression from this or that official instruction, nor for the violation of the conventional demands of human public opinion, but for every deviation from the demands of the inner voice of God, which are known and comprehensible to ourselves alone—of that God from whom we have emanated and to whom we shall return when we leave this life.

And in what light, before that court of eternal love and truth, do those men appear, who are unable to go against their consciences in taking part in military service, and whose earthly lot is at the present time in your hands? To the God of love these men naturally appear as His most faithful and obedient servants. They have believed with simplicity and whole-heartedness in the truth and immutability of those demands of love which He has Himself implanted in their hearts, and disclosed to them in the life and teaching of Jesus. These men differ from others only in having placed the divine love towards man higher than everything else, and having become so penetrated with its spirit and obligations that they can in no way consent either to kill, or to learn to kill their fellow-beings. The will of God has become more binding to them than anything else in the world, and they have gone to prison, to martyrdom, to death — solely that they may not transgress the demands of this divine love, by which they live. They cannot enter the military service for the simple reason that already they are in the service of Him who teaches them to love their enemies, and who taught humanity that "no murderer hath eternal life abiding in him" (Matt. v. 44; 1 John iii. 15).

And what is our position before this Supreme Court of God in relation to these men? We can only, in the presence of God, while humbly acknowledging the purity and saintliness of the motives of these His children, thank them for the light with which they illumine the darkness around us, for the true love with which they warm our frozen hearts. In the eyes of God these men manifestly suffer for us; they undergo torture for love of their neighbour, *i.e.* of me, of you, of all who are dear to us. How then can we fail to recognise our sacred duty before God, to do all in our power to afford them that support which they, as men, cannot at times but need, and to alleviate their sufferings, the weight of which must sometimes be almost beyond their strength?

That movement towards universal brotherhood in which these men are taking part, is daily developing in breadth and depth. From all sides—as from Russia so also from other countries—joyous tidings keep reaching us of fresh cases of similar refusals to perform military service, in consequence of its incompatibility with the ripening demands of the human conscience. Of the ultimate triumph of the Christian ideal of love and goodwill between men I cannot doubt, and I feel certain that, if not we oureslves, our posterity, is destined to take part in the establishment of this new era in the life of mankind. Those first intimations of the approaching dawn at which we, with you, have the joy to be present, bear witness to the inevitable coming of the perfect day. And succeeding generations, while enjoying the welfare of general disarmament and peace, will bless the memory of the martyrs, who are at this moment sacrificing themselves before our eyes, in order to help forward the coming of that time. Let us then be worthy of that which is taking place around us—let us do the utmost in our power to mitigate the martyrdom of these men who are announcing to us the approaching amelioration of mutual human relations. And above all, let us try to understand and accomplish that which is, in the present case, demanded of us by God.

Pardon me, sir, for having, in appealing to you on behalf of these men who, on account of their aspirations and their position, have become infinitely dear to me, given free expression to that which fills my heart at the thought of their condition. Knowing that at the present time their lot lies directly in your hands, I could not refrain from writing this letter, which I request you to accept in the same spirit of sincere goodwill in which I write it. . . .

November 1st, 1896.

Brotherhood Publishing Company's Publications

In Preparation.]

THE CHRISTIAN TEACHING.

By

Leo Tolstoy.

[*To be Issued Shortly.*

A brief, condensed, and systematic statement of the Conception of Life which constitutes the teaching of Jesus.

By Leo Tolstoy.

▲ ▲ ▲

Crown 8vo, art linen, gilt top, price 6s. each.

Pp. xxxi–368.

THE FOUR GOSPELS HARMONISED AND TRANSLATED.

PART I.

CONTENTS.

I. THE INCARNATION OF THE INTELLIGENCE OF LIFE.
II. THE NEW LIFE: REJECTION OF THE JEWISH GOD.
III. THE KINGDOM OF GOD.
IV. THE LAW: SERMON ON THE MOUNT.
INDICES.

Pp. vi–376.

THE FOUR GOSPELS HARMONISED AND TRANSLATED.

PART II.

CONTENTS.

V. THROUGH FULFILMENT OF THE LAW WE HAVE TRUE LIFE.
VI. MAN SHALL NOT LIVE BY BREAD ALONE.
VII. TESTIMONY TO THE TRUTH OF CHRIST'S DOCTRINE.
VIII. NO OTHER LIFE.
INDICES.

THE BROTHERHOOD PUBLISHING COMPANY, CROYDON.

By Leo Tolstoy—*continued*.

✦ ✦ ✦

In Preparation.]

THE FOUR GOSPELS HARMONISED AND TRANSLATED.

PART III.

CONTENTS.

IX. TEMPTATIONS.
X. WRESTLING WITH TEMPTATIONS.
XI. WHAT WE LEARN FROM THE LIFE OF JESUS.
XII. VICTORY OF THE SPIRIT.

This great work, written eighteen years ago, d.. ..ot see the light in print until the appearance of the first Russian edition at Geneva, last year. Probably it was the faultiness of that edition, in addition to previous incorrect and mutilated versions of his works, which caused COUNT TOLSTOY to announce that in future he would give his written sanction to all editions and translations which he considered faithful to the originals written by him. That sanction is accorded to the present translation of "The Four Gospels," as will be seen from the facsimile of the author's letter appearing in Part I.

The Works of TOLSTOY, "What I Believe," "My Confession," "The Kingdom of God is within You," "Life," and others, it is already evident, mark an epoch in religious thought, and a new departure in, or rather reversion to, the Christian life. Those works are based upon the free and profound study of the Gospels, the results of which we are now enabled to give to the English-speaking public. Strauss himself was not more drastic in his historical criticism of the Gospels than Tolstoy; yet no writer could transcend Tolstoy in his submission to the simple doctrines as to the conduct of life, taught by Jesus. It is not too much to say that this book is essential to those who earnestly desire true light on the Christian Gospel, and who are concerned to know how the Gospel stands in relation to the world in our own times.

THE BROTHERHOOD PUBLISHING COMPANY, CROYDON.

By Leo Tolstoy—continued.

♣ ♣ ♣

Crown 8vo, art linen, gilt top, price 2s.

WORK WHILE YE HAVE THE LIGHT.

A story of early Christianity, illustrating the Christian Solution of Social Problems — Labour, Property, Government, Marriage, Art, etc. An excellent introduction to Tolstoy's later writings.

Demy 8vo, pp. x-384, price 5s.

CHRIST'S CHRISTIANITY.

I.—HOW I CAME TO BELIEVE; Otherwise, "My Confession."

II.—WHAT I BELIEVE; Otherwise, "My Religion."

III.—THE SPIRIT OF CHRIST'S TEACHING.

This Volume contains Three Separate Works, which together give a comprehensive view of the Author's Social and Religious Teaching.

Each, crown 8vo, cloth, price 2s. 6d.

WHAT TO DO?

THE KINGDOM OF GOD IS WITHIN YOU; or, Christianity not as a Mystical Doctrine, but as a New Life-Conception.

THE GOSPEL IN BRIEF.

BOYHOOD. A Story.
Of autobiographical interest.

SEVASTOPOL.

WAR AND PEACE. Four Vols.

ANNA KARÉNINA. 3s. 6d.
With Ten Illustrations by PAUL FRÉNZENY, and Photogravure Portrait of the Author.

THE BROTHERHOOD PUBLISHING COMPANY, CROYDON.

By Leo Tolstoy—*continued*.

♣ ♣ ♣

Each, crown 8vo, cloth, price 2s. 6d.

IVAN ILYITCH, and other Stories.

KREUTZER SONATA and FAMILY HAPPINESS.

BOOKLETS. New Editions Revised. Small 12mo, cloth, with Embossed Design on Cover, each containing Two Drawings by H. R. MILLAR. In Box, price 2s. each.

Vol. I.—WHERE LOVE IS, THERE GOD IS ALSO.
  The Godson.

Vol. II.—WHAT MEN LIVE BY.
  What Shall it Profit a Man?

Vol. III.—THE TWO PILGRIMS.
  If You Neglect the Fire, You Don't Put it Out.

Vol. IV.—MASTER AND MAN.

Vol. V.—THREE PARABLES. (Cloth only.)

May also be had separately, in paper cover, price 1s. each.

"We hope that these little books, presented in the most captivating of forms, will have the circulation among Englishmen which they deserve."—*Athenæum.*

♣ ♣ ♣

By John C. Kenworthy.

Each, crown 8vo, paper, 1s.; cloth, 2s.

THE ANATOMY OF MISERY:
  Plain Lectures in Economics.

THE CHRISTIAN REVOLT.
  Signs of the Coming Commonwealth.

THE BROTHERHOOD PUBLISHING COMPANY, CROYDON.

By *John C. Kenworthy*—continued.

❧ ❧ ❧

Crown 8vo, paper 1s., cloth 2s.
FROM BONDAGE TO BROTHERHOOD.
A Message to the Workers.

Crown 8vo, cloth, price 2s. 6d.
THE WORLD'S LAST PASSAGE.

Crown 8vo, with Portrait, price 6d. net.
A PILGRIMAGE TO TOLSTOY.

❧ ❧ ❧

Crown 8vo, cloth, 2s.
By *Michael Flürscheim.*
THE REAL HISTORY OF MONEY-ISLAND. A Story of To-Day.

❧ ❧ ❧

Paper cover, 6d.
THE TSAR'S CORONATION, *As seen by* De MONTE ALTO.
A vivid account of the recent great ceremony at Moscow and its accompanying disaster.

THE BROTHERHOOD PUBLISHING COMPANY, CROYDON.

Price 2d. each; by post, 2½d.

The
Brotherhood Series of Pamphlets.

A Series, partly specially written, and partly selected, comprising short pieces, which frankly, clearly, and radically apply the gospel teaching to the social and individual life of to-day.

BY JOHN C. KENWORTHY.

I.—SLAVERY: Ancient and Modern.
II.—TOLSTOY: His Teaching and Influence in England.

BY NELLIE SHAW.

III.—SOME IMPRESSIONS OF THE SERMON ON THE MOUNT.

BY LEO TOLSTOY.

IV.—THE TRIUMPH OF LABOUR.
Other Issues to follow in this Series.

✤ ✤ ✤

Monthly, One Penny. By post, 1s. 6d. yearly.

"THE NEW ORDER."

The Journal of the Croydon Brotherhood Church. Records thought and news of the movement of practical Christian life now rising in every Christian country.

Ready Shortly, One Penny.
IVAN THE FOOL. By Leo Tolstoy.

THE BROTHERHOOD PUBLISHING COMPANY, CROYDON.

www.ingramcontent.com/pod-product-compliance
Lightning Source LLC
Chambersburg PA
CBHW030343170426
43202CB00010B/1226